Choq

A Gothic Fable

Also by Quentin Crisp

All This and Bevin Too
The Naked Civil Servant
How To Have a Life-Style
Love Made Easy

Chog

A Gothic Fable

Quentin Crisp

Illustrations by
Gahan Wilson

METHUEN

NEW YORK   LONDON   TORONTO   SYDNEY

Manufactured in the United States of America
First American Edition
Published in the United States of America by
METHUEN, INC.
733 Third Avenue
New York, New York 10017
Designed by Elaine Cox

Library of Congress in Publication Data

Crisp, Quentin
  Chog, a Gothic fable.

  I. Title.
PZ3.C86793CH   1979   [PR6005.R65]   823'.9'12   79–15617

  ISBN 0–416–00131–9   pbk.

This book is dedicated to
Mr. Lucas who wished to be involved.

Contents

Lord Emms
and His
Inheritance

Ravenage is a city only because it is built around a small cathedral, which is itself no bigger than many parish churches in larger towns. A thin, white road that glows in the dusk comes lurching, swerving across the moorland and seems to pause uncertainly in order to negotiate a bridge over a stream too narrow for barges and too swift-flowing for pleasure craft. At the junction of road and river a few houses are clustered like spectators at a street accident. The whole surrounding area was once ruled by the Emms family.

At the edge of the city the Emmses had built what it then seemed reasonable to call the Great House. It still bore that name long after other residences just as large and twice as efficient had been erected nearby. These new buildings housed the children of farmers whose land had gradually encroached upon the Emmses' demesne. At last the Emms estate dwindled to a large, awkward garden which stopped at a stream that had once run through the middle of it and which seemed so totally to have lost heart that in hot summers it became a mere ditch guarded by disgruntled nettles.

Even the garden in front of the house had shrunk. The huge iron gates that had once stood by the main road had at some time been moved back from it so that they now stood seven feet high in ludicrous grandeur between newer walls that could be climbed by an adventurous child. There was almost no drop on the inner side of these defenses because the damp soil of the sloping garden had piled up against them through the desolate years. That part of the drive that was outside the gates had become public property and had acquired large houses on it glad of the quietude that settles on a road leading only to another house. Inside the gates, the drive swept along in front of the house and widened so that in times gone by coaches could easily turn to leave or wait in large numbers all night long while their owners danced or drank or occasionally endeavored to do both. Such parties were frantically given by the first Lord Emms in the hope that one of the guests might drink enough to forget himself and propose to any of a succession of ill-favored daughters. It was bad luck and this round of revelry that had drained the resources of the Emms dynasty.

The house was wide and from the front looked bigger than it was, just as superficially its owners seemed grander than they really were. The apparent width of the edifice was increased by a disused stable which stood at one side and on the other by a conservatory which had begun to fall into ruins within ten years of its being erected. When the estate dwindled, new walls were built which reduced the width of the gardens to that of the buildings. Thereafter the only way from the back garden to the front was through the house, save for a gate at one side which only the servants used or by way of a rheumatic pergola between the main building and the greenhouse, on which even rambler roses were too ashamed to lean.

Finally the once rich and, at least heraldically speaking, noble line of landowners came to a halt in Lord Henry Emms, on whose youngest sister's dowry almost the last drop of the family fortune had been spent. By dint of dogged longevity and sheer meanness, he managed to reverse the financial ebb tide that had dragged his parents onto the rocks of penury. His lordship married for money, gradually reduced the number of his servants to two and, with the assistance of what must have been the only honest lawyer in captivity, once more became rich.

But the regained wealth did not bring back lights to the windows of the Great House as health might restore color to the cheeks of a woman. His lordship never drank wine, not because it was wicked but because water was cheaper and after the death of his parents, Lord Emms never gave another party of any kind. Many of the upper rooms were permanently shut up, and the greenhouse, once shot through like a vast diamond with lights from the drawing room, was now opaque with vegetation. Those plants which had not withered had grown unchecked until they burst through the glass roof like furious unwanted relatives buried alive.

The manservant consequently ceased to be a butler but, so that he might earn every last penny of his meager wages, he became, in a shaky sort of way, a gardener. He could sprinkle weed-killer on the gravel of the drive because murder was an occupation he enjoyed, and he could mow the lawn of the back garden. Life, however, was not his business, so he did not encourage anything to blossom. The trees and shrubs did not try to beguile the mansion's dim eyes with a display of color.

They seemed, rather, to be full of a moist, dark menace.

The attic, which ran the entire length of the building and which had once been a playroom for the hapless girls, had become too damp for human habitation as time and the angry elements scrabbled away at the tiles above it. But the walls of the house defied all threats. They were of huge blocks of stone the color of volcanic ash and, in some places, were four feet thick. Their function was to make sure that Lord Emms's life was never invaded by anything remotely like gaiety.

Behind these fortifications lived his lordship under self-imposed house arrest. His only glimpse of nature was in the domesticated form of his garden, which occasionally he surveyed from the safe distance of the arbor—a flagstoned space covered by a glass roof just outside the drawing-room window.

He was indeed growing old, but he had adopted a routine as limited as if he were ancient. So that no money need be wasted on warming the rest of the house, his waking hours were spent in one room, usually the library, where he read about the past; he shunned all literature that described the contemporary world of King Edward and Mrs. George Keppel, of the Marquis de Soveral and Lord Esher, of Mrs. Pankhurst and her suffragettes, lest he be tempted to go out and investigate it. When not occupied with a book, he wrote long letters to his lawyer, his brokers, and to relatives, asking them not to visit him. In an effort to break the monotony of his existence, he consumed four tiny meals a day. Since the dining room was at the other end of the house, to reach it he crossed the hall wearing a woolen shawl around this thin shoulders, walking like someone going uphill on skis. Although he had chosen this narrow life, he must have felt his loneliness, because he kept various pets, king among which was a half-grown, part-time German shepherd called Fido.

Many long, dark years before Lord Emms had graduated to this degree of eccentricity—when he was only an Hon.—his father and mother had directed his wandering attention to the daughter of the rich farmer who now tilled what had once been their land. This they did partly from a desire for revenge but mainly in a feverish effort to stem the fiscal tide that was washing them into bankruptcy. To the villagers, the young man seemed touchingly filial, but in fact, though he was hysterically obstinate in small matters, he longed for all major decisions to be made for him by others—even, if necessary, by his parents. He avoided looking into the uncertain future and, apart from having to endure his father's nagging sarcasm, lived snugly enough in the continuous present. Preferring to concentrate on problems of his own, he gave no thought to the troubles of the world, to the German naval menace, to the Russian encroachments in northern Persia, to Dr. Crippen and his ghastly deeds, or even to the misfortunes of his neighbors.

The courting couple dawdled in the field of poppies that lay between her father's farm and the Great House, and although he thought her a brutish young woman, he realized that he would never be able to defile his hands with her money without also defiling them with her person. Finally one Sunday afternoon he found the strength to traverse the acres of un-leavened flesh that lay between him and solvency; he felt like a gold prospector in the Klondike, except that the terrain was warmer.

He could not conceal his disgust, and for this his sweet-heart never forgave him. She got her own back by marrying him, and almost immediately burdened him with a son and a daughter. The boy lived to the tantalizing age of eleven; the girl could only manage to stick it out for two weeks, after which she departed for a world which may not have been better but could hardly have been worse. The young Lord Emms did not grieve; he had not wanted children, for in his opinion they were noisy and expensive. Nevertheless, when they were gone, he used their deaths to taunt his wife. Her blood group was rhesus negative. Informed of this by the doctor, he took to calling her "my monkey wife." If she had understood this merry quip, she might have been more distressed than she was, but in truth she comprehended very little of her husband's humor. She had received none but that basic education which comes from watching the coupling of farm animals, and, in any case, she paid very little attention to anything he said.

Toward the end of her life she realized that she did miss having someone with whom to converse and, to correct this deficiency, acquired a parrot. Although very young, the bird rapidly learned to say "Horrid Henry" and many other pleas-ing phrases that it satisfied her ladyship to hear. She made not the slightest effort to be her husband's equal in anything but the intensity of her hatred. They moved about the house like hens in a courtyard, totally ignoring one another even at meal-times, though then, for the convenience of the servants, they shared the same room.

Lady Emms could have remained in the ring just as long as her adversary but, twelve years after the death of her son, she died mysteriously of food poisoning.

When his wife was in her grave, Lord Emms regretted having called her his monkey wife. The title, he decided, was too good for her. In those days he still occasionally went out into the world, though usually to meet animals rather than human beings. On one such excursion he purchased a monkey, which, in order to mock his wife even in her grave, he named St. Agnes. He took to declaring to the few acquaintances who still insisted on calling on him that he preferred the society of his four-footed companions to that of people. As he expatiated on this subject he would caress the ears of one of Fido's pred-ecessors. The dog would stretch himself languorously and sigh. When this performance had been repeated often enough, most callers took the broad hint and, as the years went by, his lordship was visited less and less by mere bipeds. His preference for furred, feathered, and even scaled creatures was derived, as it always must be, from the fact that, with the exception of his wife's parrot, they never answered back or tried to cheer him up. The latter response annoyed Lord Emms even more than contradiction.

It was on this same principle that he tolerated the

Davieses. Though they did not know it, it was not their
efficiency, of which they held an exaggerated view, but their
meekness and their pessimism that were the qualities by means
of which they finally survived all the other members of the
domestic staff at the Great House. From dawn till dusk and
long after it, they fetched and carried for their superiors in the
kitchen. After the death of Lady Emms, their functions were
merely to feed their master and his menagerie and to keep the
house just as it was the day her ladyship died. Lord Emms
wished to be perpetually reminded of that happy event.

When, within a month of one another, they had entered
the service of his parents, the Hon. Henry had not long been
married. The Davieses were only a few years his junior but,
though they were young, they were never youthful. This fact
appealed to their employers, and that they were not married
was further recommendation. Among the lower orders wed-
lock tended to lead to pregnancy and the loss of working hours.
The Davieses had not entered into matrimony because, at that
time, their position had not seemed desperate enough to war-
rant a measure so extreme. Lord and Lady Emms senior were
stern but not vindictive, and it was not until they were both
dead that the Davieses felt the urgent need to pool their resources if they were to survive the long, hard climb through the
hierarchic structure of the domestic staff. Although serious
trouble never came from the new Lady Emms, whose hatred
aimed directly and solely at her husband, seldom missing its
mark, the new Lord Emms' venom was ejaculated like

buckshot. Never a day went by but one or another of the servants was wounded by it.

Davies was like a pencil drawing of his master, executed on parchment by an indifferent artist. In his youth Lord Emms had been a slight, filleted young man with floppy hair, a pink-and-white complexion, and lips a shade too red, a degree too moist. In middle age the willowy stance became a stoop, the gliding gait a shuffle, the luscious locks a desert waste. It was at this stage that Davies felt sufficiently confident to begin imitating his master. He too started to walk slowly with his head in advance of his chest. The posture seemed to him the essence of refinement. He also adopted a rasping voice but, whereas his lordship occasionally shouted or at least emitted a loud croak, his servant seldom raised his voice above a whisper. It always seemed as though "Lunch is served" was news too important for any but his master's ears. If he had stood opposite Lord Emms, they would have appeared to be about to kiss. Perhaps for this reason, Davies invariably placed himself at right angles to his employer and spoke into an imaginary grave open at their feet.

Mrs. Davies had never thought of imitating her mistress. She knew it did not befit her station in life. From the cradle to the tomb her manner remained childlike, apologetic while faintly affronted. Like her husband, she too was of sallow complexion, but chronic irritation had traced a web of tiny lines across his face. So it looked as though it were made of cracked ice, while on her heavier countenance time and grief had dragged the fat of her cheeks downward until the eyes were overhung like those of a St. Bernard and the lips were bracketed with superfluous flesh. In contrast to his, her hair remained eternally springy and, even in age, was only faintly streaked with white, but that may have been because it was so seldom washed. Possibly for the same reason, beneath her perpetual black serge dress, her ivory body remained waxy and, by the standards of her day, beautiful, but no one ever saw it and, after a few lean years of marriage, it was never touched.

When it finally arrived, the triumph of the Davieses was not without a little irony. As housekeepers, looking down from the pinnacle of their profession, they saw that what had started out as a marathon with a large number of contestants had finished as a walk-over; they were alone on the track with no losers behind them on whom to vent that rage which is the result of years of accumulated fatigue. The annihilation of their adversaries was partly the result of Lord Emms' passion for economy, but it was also due to the fact that the will to serve was beginning to go out of fashion. The Davieses were dimly aware of this. If, when questioned by outsiders about life at the Great House, they said that they ironed the newspapers before presenting them to their employer or that they washed the change from his trousers pockets, their hearers shook with bucolic laughter, and Davies was openly mocked for his neat appearance and his refinements of diction.

Once they were in sole command of their kingdom, the Davieses worked with greater and greater zeal. They did this not because their feelings toward Lord Emms had mellowed but because, with each passing year, they thought they saw improvements in their chances of receiving a legacy. It was with barely concealed glee that to some luckless caller they relayed a message from their master's own lips that he was out. With equal eagerness they carried every black-edged letter immediately after it fell on the hall mat to whatever room his lordship was occupying. Later in the day the contents of the wastepaper basket of that particular room were pieced together on the kitchen table like a jigsaw puzzle. From the reassembled fragments Davies tried to ascertain how dear a friend or how close a relative the deceased had been. In this way, to his amazement, he learned that something had been left to Lord Emms. To his increased amazement, the bequest was a dog called Fido.

When told what train to meet and what freight to expect, Davies expressed polite surprise. It was a cold day and every new pet meant added work, but he set off for Ravenage station without a murmur. Since his master had never had any intention of parting with the large sums of money required to buy animals with pedigrees, all his canine friends were mongrels. In this respect, Fido was no exception, but he had transcended his doubtful origins by the unusual alertness of his gaze and the dignity of his deportment. What Davies saw through the waiting-room window was certainly the most impressive of dogs, regardless of breeding. He was of sturdy build with short fur as pale as the hide of a Jersey cow and eyes the color of

gooseberries, and he was so innocent that, when he was introduced to Davies, he wagged his tail. When they left the station,
snow had begun to fall and they walked home together amica-
bly with Davies dutifully holding his umbrella over the dog.
Sad to say, in spite of his spectacular appearance and his agree-
able disposition, it was this animal, or rather his owner's unusual attitude toward it, that drove the Davieses to their first act
of desperation.

Lord Emms treated all his other pets with affability
marred by a faint element of condescension, but to the new dog
he spoke as to an equal—nay, a superior. He sought its protection. "You look after me," he was heard to say, "and I'll look
after you." To most people this would be a harmless enough
remark. To the Davieses it was full of foreboding. It was they,
not Lord Emms, who looked after all the pets. According to the
needs of each creature, they fed or cleaned or exercised it. In
their minds, the only way it was possible for his owner to look
after Fido was financially.

Once they had decided that this interpretation of their
employer's words was the true one, every incident involving
the dog seemed to confirm their fears. One afternoon some
children scrambled through the hedge at the end of the back
garden. The day was part of a false spring that had lured Lord
Emms into sitting in the arbor in a huge cane chair that Davies
had carried thither for him. When he caught sight of the
urchins, he cursed them. They could not possibly have had any
previous knowledge of his lordship, because to explain their

presence they said they were collecting items for a rummage sale. Even if it had not been an unlikely time of year for such an event, no excuse could have made them less welcome. "Guard the house," Davies heard his master shout. He knew by the warm enthusiasm with which the command was given that it was not addressed to him. Fido, who had until this moment been wagging his tail at the children, bounded toward them with mock ferocity so convincing that the intruders screamed and scampered away. When, his mission accomplished, the dog returned and laid his head between his owner's knees, he was greeted with praise and a pat on the head. "Later on," said Lord Emms, "we must get you some puppies so that you and your descendants can look after this house forever." Then, bending toward the animal's trembling nose, in a voice so low that although Davies held his breath he could hardly hear it, his lordship added, "Even when I'm gone."

The Davieses sensed that their master's pets were their rivals in a very practical sense. They had never doubted the sincerity of his often-expressed preference for animal companionship. In small ways it had blighted every day of their existence. Now they foresaw that it might also utterly change that future about which, without any evidence to support their feelings, they had begun recently to be tremulously optimistic.

The Davieses
Go Into
Action

The Davieses were frightened but, as yet, they made no definite plan to save themselves. Their employer's demise still seemed such a long way off. The Davieses could easily work out for themselves how old his lordship was, but they were hypnotized by appearances. Like many people who in youth had a pale, pinched look and lost their hair prematurely, Lord Emms' compensation came with his advancing years: having never looked young, in old age his appearance reflected very little of the cruel passage of time. Except for a certain deafness, he seemed not to have suffered any dimming of his faculties in twenty-five years. Even his loss of hearing, in the estimation of people who knew him well, might merely have been a ruse to avoid having to take notice of the opinions of others. All the same, although from the outside he seemed hideously eternal, within he must have felt some intimations of mortality. In a letter so thick that while even holding it before a lamp Davies could not decipher a word of its contents, he asked his lawyer to visit him so that he might alter his will. The addressee was a certain Mr. Minguillan—not the trusted adviser who had helped him to regain his fortune but that man's son-in-law, a slightly sinister being whose firm grasp of financial matters might be judged by the size of his fees. As always, the Davieses were told nothing about the expected visitor except his name and that he would arrive at four o'clock, that being the hour at which hospitality is traditionally least expensive.

When, upon opening the front door to the stranger, Mrs. Davies saw the briefcase under his arm, though she tried to keep her face an inscrutable ivory mask, her heart became deeply agitated. She was glad to be able to turn away and lead him to the library, where Lord Emms dozed before an undernourished fire with Fido stretched across the hearth rug. In a feeble effort to discover the nature of the gentleman's mission, Mrs. Davies announced him as the doctor. "Doctor," his lordship croaked. "I sent for no damned doctor. I can bring about my death myself if necessary. Oh, it's you." The ploy worked only insofar as it proved that Mr. Minguillan was not a physician. Having closed the door discreetly, Mrs. Davies hurried to the scullery. There she put on her galoshes and, going out of the side door, ran around the house. Outside the library she was nearly involved in a head-on collision with her husband, who had circumnavigated the building from the opposite direction. Beneath the partially open window they flattened the crocuses with the formidable weight of their curiosity.

They found that they could hear distinctly only the visitor's words, because it was he who felt compelled to shout. Inevitably his remarks formed the smaller part of the conversation. Nevertheless, the eavesdroppers came to the unshakable conclusion that their dark suspicions were true. Their master intended to leave all his money to the wretched pets that fouled the air of the house and defiled its floors and furnishings. Their own names they heard mentioned only in a mumbled parenthesis.

It was a long interview and, for the Davieses, very uncomfortable. When the visitor had gone, they stamped the mud from their boots and, sitting by the fire, tried to thaw the rheumatism from their knees. Then they prepared their master's evening meal. This, as ever, they served to him at one end of a table at which twenty guests could easily have dined— though, naturally, no gathering so lavish had occurred in the Great House since the previous Lord Emms had died. Not until the diminutive coffee cup had been cleared away and washed up did the Davieses sit down to their own supper. Eating with far more delicacy than their employer, they conversed in whispers without even noticing they were doing so.

"But we don't know, do we?" asked Mrs. Davies in tones of muted anguish. "We don't know anything for certain." In times gone by, she had relied on her husband's knowledge of the world to solve all her problems. Her trust had not always been wisely placed. Now, for lack of anyone else to turn to, she still addressed herself to him, but her remarks were really more in the nature of a generalized cry of despair—like letters to *The Times,* though not so well composed.

"We have a very shrewd hidea," Davies replied. "I've voiced my suspicions more than once recently." In moments of grave importance, he was in the habit of inserting a few haphazard aspirates into his pronouncements, as a bad pianist uses the loud pedal.

"What shall we do? What ever shall we do?"

"Nothing hasty," Davies answered. He was being made

uneasy by the degree of emotion already audible in his wife's voice. "We have plenty of time—maybe years."

"How do you know? He doesn't look any worse, but something must be wrong. If he wasn't feeling poorly, he wouldn't have sent for That One."

"Don't get excited. That's the worst thing to do. If we act without due deliberation, we may . . ." Davies faltered. He couldn't bring himself to say "get the sack." Instead he substituted, "draw suspicion upon ourselves."

"Suspicion of what?" This question, to which Mrs. Davies already knew the answer, was met with nothing more than a significant look. This silenced her for some time. Then she said, "But even if there wasn't a single animal in the place, we don't know that we'd get anything. We don't *know*."

"You're a fat lot of help, I must say," Davies snorted. "We've just got to do our honest best. No one can do more than that," he added with a hint of self-satisfaction.

They started on the tortoise; it looked so like their employer. Having foolishly just emerged from hibernation, it was easily found wandering in the neglected kitchen garden. The Davieses carried it into the coal shed, where, it not being in Mr. Davies' nature to do anything violent, he merely turned it over, while his wife's share of the labor was to raise the coal axe high above her head and aim a terrible blow at the wretched reptile's stomach. It was not the kind of work for which she could be said to have a flair. At the last moment she shut her eyes. Her aim fell short of the mark, the blow merely flipping the tortoise over like a counter in a game of tiddlywinks. Mr. Davies grabbed his victim and they tried again. He was unusually patient with his wife's ineptitude. This was because, in a small way, he was a hunter. He would not have minded if this pastime had taken up most of the afternoon. His wish was not granted. Chiefly because she could bear no more, Mrs. Davies' next blow was fatal.

When her victim's legs had waved a last faint farewell to life, Mrs. Davies pointed out to her husband that they were doing precisely what he had warned her that they must not do. They were acting without due deliberation. Mr. Davies agreed. Their rivals must not be eliminated in this boisterous fashion, but ingeniously. Their deaths must be contrived to look like accidents and their remains must be shown, or at least be capable of being shown, to their master. The many possibilities of this scheme appealed greatly to Davies' imagination. It was too late to invent a plausible explanation for the fate of the tortoise. It was buried in the dead of night under one of the flagstones of the arbor. Mrs. Davies was horrified to notice that, for days afterward, whenever he was let out into the garden, Fido would pay his respects to the dear departed by putting his nose to the reptile's tombstone and uttering a wan funeral oration. From time to time she saw him slowly scrape his claws across the unmarked grave.

Davies decided that, for the sake of decorum, a few weeks should be allowed to elapse between each stage of the final solution. It was, therefore, not until March that, with the aid of a colander, he took one occupant a day from the fish tank, placed it for ten minutes on the previous day's copy of *The Times,* and then replaced it in a less rarefied element. When the contents of the tank were more dead than alive, Lord Emms remarked upon this fact. He displayed curiosity but no emotion. So far the Davieses were making smoother progress than they had dared to hope—but the greatest demands had not yet been made, either on his ingenuity or her fortitude.

April was the cruelest month. It was devoted to the cat.

Once in a lifetime everyone meets someone he can loathe with all his heart without reserve and without hindrance. Indeed, life would be almost intolerable if this were not the case. For a few unfortunate souls the object of their detestation is unattainable. It may even be someone who is never seen—a man who coughs at dawn in the next room or, in the bathroom, sings the wrong words to a well-known song. Other, luckier mortals find their lives fortuitously interwoven with those of the people they hate; they meet them every day at work or find them attending the same lectures at a university. Occasionally a couple are utterly welded together by the flame of their mutual antipathy; they marry.

Davies was a humble man; he did not aspire to loathing another human being. It would have seemed presumptuous. He settled for the cat and, what bliss!, his passion was returned a hundredfold.

This longtime adversary had no name. It was a tarnished black in color, wore its ears like bicycle handles, and was as slinky as the shadow of a thief. It robbed without need and killed without mercy. It had the step of a dancer and the voice of a demented prima donna.

In the days when he had first found himself a gardener by default, Davies had made a few stylized efforts to fulfill the functions of that calling. From the dining-room window, the cat would watch him through slit eyes the color of bile. As soon as the man's back was turned, the animal would rush out and, curving its spine in an ecstasy of diabolical glee, would pour its hydrochloric scorn on the newly planted cuttings. When the weather was not suitable for gardening and Davies worked indoors, the cat would catch a mouse or a bird and drag the entrails of its half-dead victim over the newly polished floors. Once, in a positive orgasm of hatred, it had gambled a few of its lives in an attempt to outbid a rival who it knew had but one. At dusk, before the lamps had been lit, it lay where it was unlikely to be seen on the stairs. The very second it felt a cautious boot upon its fur, it sprang up, causing Davies to falter and lose his footing. Having brought off this coup, the animal leaped over his falling foe and rushed screaming into the hall. The only words of concern uttered by Lord Emms were, "Davies. Stop tormenting that cat."

Sometimes, when Davies was sitting by the kitchen fire, he would draw the corners of his mouth downward and back with such force that his facial muscles ached. Seeing his features contorted in this way, his wife would ask, "What's the matter, for heaven's sake?" Davies would look up startled. "What?

Nothing," he would reply. But he had been thinking about the
cat.

Now at last he need no longer waste his time with idle
daydreams. The hour had arrived for the making of plans that
were capable of actual fulfillment. Davies decided that it would
look best if it appeared that the hated creature had been run
over. Knowing his enemy well, he first put on a pair of thick
gardening gloves. Then, so that nothing need be wasted, he
put the last surviving fish into a sack, which he opened invit-
ingly in front of the cat. The animal paused for a moment,
sensing that there was danger, but it could not resist the bait. As
soon as it was in the sack, Davies lifted it up so that his wife, who
had been waiting like an operating-theater nurse, could tie the
opening with a piece of tarred string. It was as well that these
maneuvers were carried out in a potting shed far from the
house. The noise was blood-curdling. Davies himself added to
its volume, for he did not survive unscathed. To restore a
decorous silence, and because she was the stronger of the two,
Mrs. Davies fetched the garden roller.

This apparent accident did evoke revulsion in his lordship. With Fido as ever beside him, he was standing in the
drawing room looking out through the open French windows
when, walking as though to a dead march, Davies came into
view. He was carrying the remains of the cat on the piece of
sackcloth in which it had met its fate. "It's our little friend, I'm
afraid," he announced in a lugubrious tone.

The dog understood the situation before his master and

moved forward to investigate. To restrain the animal's curios-ity, Lord Emms knelt down and placed his arms around its neck. "God curse all drivers," he hissed.

"I'm afraid it's those horseless carriages, my lord," Davies explained. "They go at such a breakneck speed."

"All vehicles whatsoever," said his employer emphatically. "Curse them all."

"Shall I bury it?" Davies asked after a respectful interval.

"At the end of the garden," his lordship replied, "and deep." As he added this, he patted Fido's head.

What with a baby anaconda to deal with, a marmoset, and two mongrel dogs much smaller than Fido, it was early autumn before the Davieses got around to the parrot. They had long since forgotten that this bird had been the companion of Lady Emms. They were, therefore, taken by surprise when, having consumed a large helping of birdseed laced with phosphorus, it cried out, "Murderer!"

The sound was so piercing that even Lord Emms heard it. Though midnight had struck some time ago, he struggled out of bed and tottered from his room to the top of the stairs. "You can't sleep any better than I do, can you, Agnes?" he crowed. The Davieses had carried the birdcage downstairs and, not expecting any dramatic effects, had neglected to shut the kitchen door. Staring into the darkness of the hall, they stood transfixed with terror.

"And you can't keep quiet about it—even in your grave," they heard their master say.

With these words he fell headlong down the stairs.

Before the funeral, Fido, who had not been feeling well for some days, sprawled across the foot of the four-poster bed on which the body of his master lay with hands folded and features free at last of that irritation which had so often furrowed them in life. In the hall were several of Mr. Landseer's famous engravings of man's faithful friend, and these may have influenced the dog's behavior.

On the day the funeral took place, a wisp of black crepe was wound about the dog's gold collar and with great dignity he stood beside the open grave in the mauve autumn rain.

Afterward, during the reading of the will, the dog became restless and put his forepaws on the arm of Mr. Minguillan's chair. Mrs. Davies rose at once to put an end to this unseemly behavior, but the lawyer merely stroked the animal's neck and went on reading.

The words he uttered caused the Davieses' blood to run cold. (It had been tepid at the best of times.) From the beginning they had foreseen that disposing of Fido, who was growing to the size of a tiger, would be a long and difficult business. The week before Lord Emms' death they had begun to meet this challenge. Now they realized that they had been within a month at most of destroying what little benefit this hateful document was ever going to afford them. Their reward for a lifetime of faithful—nay, cringing—service was that they were to be permitted to remain in this cold and well-nigh impossible-to-manage house at their present paltry wages for

as long as they conscientiously attended to the needs of whatever animals were living at the time of their master's death.
When the last of these died, the remaining income from the
entire estate was to be used to convert the Great House into a
veterinary institute whose function would be to carry out ex-
periments on human beings in the hope of discovering cures
for animal diseases.

Fido Comes
Into His Own

Sitting on the opposite side of the long dining-room table, the Davieses bowed their heads before the barrage of numerals that issued from the lawyer's lips. They dared not even look at one another for fear that some expression of rage or hate might cross their faces. They accepted their fate without question and without protest, both knowing that they had become quite unfit to confront the outside world. What superficial contact they had been forced to have with it in Ravenage had showed them that, while they had remained the same, all else had become strange beyond recognition—almost beyond endurance.

As soon as he had finished reading the will, Mr. Minguillan congratulated the Davieses on their good fortune and handed them their wages, augmented by a sum that he thought appropriate as an allowance for the dog.

Overnight their attitude toward Fido changed. He had already been given an exploratory dose of arsenic. This had made him liable to bouts of diarrhea. Yesterday, when one of these bouts seemed imminent, Davies, cursing in a genteel manner, had dragged him by the collar to the scullery door and ejected him. Today the Davieses' subservience which had brought out the worst in Lord Emms was lavished upon the dog. His slightest change of mood was greeted with cooing sounds. His furry brow was soothed, and he was invited to lie on the rag rug before the kitchen fire where once his vast bulk had been considered a nuisance.

At first Fido reacted favorably to this sudden solicitude. He wagged his tail and cast liquid glances toward his benefactors from his gooseberry-colored eyes. Just as formerly he had spent every waking hour in the company of Lord Emms, now he followed Mrs. Davies from room to room, watching her every movement as she dusted the china ornaments on the mantelshelves or peeled vegetables in the scullery. Whenever she stood still, he leaned against her thigh.

One day, when she was washing some watercress in the colander and thinking about the murdered fishes, he nudged her with his long flank so persistently that her considerable bulk was displaced. She waited for a moment and then moved back to her original position. Again the dog pressed his body against her thigh. Again she moved back, this time giving Fido a sidelong glance and smiling. The jostling had become a game. Suddenly she knelt down and hugged her playmate. He put his forepaws across her shoulders so heavily that she toppled backward. For a moment she lay on the scullery floor with her legs in the air while the dog stood over her wagging his tail and skittishly defying her to get up. At this moment, Davies unexpectedly entered the room. "What's going on?" he asked prudishly. "What's he doing?"

"Nothing," his wife replied nervously. "Nothing at all." For a single sentence her country accent returned. "We was just 'aving a bit of a lark. That's all."

"Then why are you crying?"

Mrs. Davies had no idea that tears had come into her eyes.

She got laboriously to her feet and brushed her skirt fore and aft with a broad hand. Then she returned to her work at the sink, glad for a time to have her back toward her husband. She felt foolish and confused. Playing with the dog, she had experienced a mood that, during the next few weeks, would recur at first frequently and then less and less often until finally it came no more. Like the fitful sunlight that sometimes raced over the dreary moorland north of Ravenage, the notion flitted across her mind that she might once again be happy—as happy as she had been in childhood before she had ever gone into service. Their master was now Mr. Minguillan, who, though more dreaded than Lord Emms because he was less familiar, would seldom appear more than once a month. Whatever mistakes she might make could always be put right, or at least smoothed over, before his next visit. The shadow of day-to-day reprimands under which she had lived so much of her life might now disappear. There was no need to think of Fido as their jailer. At the very worst he was merely a silent bailiff for their new landlord. Why should they fear him? Why should he not be drawn by kindess into collusion with them? In her imagination rose the vision of her husband standing in the scullery doorway waiting for everything to be restored to that order that he knew and loved. The sunlight faded from her mind; the storm clouds rolled on toward the horizon.

Mrs. Davies knew that she could never safely mention any of these feelings to her husband; she did not know the words with which to present them convincingly. She had learned, in any case, that nothing annoyed him more than the mention of happiness. Mr. Davies was a pessimist because his employer had been one. To Mrs. Davies, Lord Emms' perpetual carping was like the weather. During waking hours she never removed her mackintosh of humility but, against all odds, she believed that elsewhere the sky might be blue. Davies regarded his late employer as deliberately tyrannical, and he was glad that he was dead. Nevertheless, he had admired him simply because he was well-born, well-heeled, and worldly. He had accepted his lordship's judgments not because he imagined that they had been thought out with any special care but because they were the opinions of a man who had been to a university. If Lord Emms had said that all men were enemies and women were archenemies, then this must be so. He was determined to regard Fido as his superior because the dog was now rich. Unlike his wife, he regarded Mr. Minguillan, who, after all was said and done, worked for his living, as a fellow servant of this sacred animal, only a notch higher than a manservant on the scale of servitude.

Mr. Davies automatically distrusted Mr. Minguillan, and, as it happened, he was right to do so. What he could not grasp, because his mind would not stretch that far, was that the lawyer greatly preferred the present disposition of his late client's wealth to what might become of it if Fido were to die. Lord Emms had not felt contempt or any other strong emotion for the Davieses. To him, at their very worst, they were like two hinges that creaked, like two clocks that lost time, like two taps that dripped. It was Mr. Minguillan who despised them. He did so because he must. In a small way he intended to cheat them by using their timidity for his own ends. They would not have sufficient technical knowledge to audit, even in their hearts, the ways in which he was about to manipulate the estate of which he was now trustee. The board and staff of a veterinary institute would be very different people to deal with. They could express doubts, utter censures, start inquiries. In a perverse way, the Davieses' enemy was on their side. Their continued existence was also his.

At the heart of this complicated situation stood the dog, bewildered and at first disoriented by the death of his master. In puppyhood he had been merely tolerated. His first owner, a distant relative of Lord Emms', had been appalled by Fido's mother mating beneath her. The rest of the litter that had been the outcome of this misalliance had been quickly distributed among his more sentimental acquaintances. Fido was retained only because he was more alert and stronger than his siblings. When this man died, his sister, though she thought the bequest of a dog quite absurd, was glad to carry out her brother's wish, and conveyed the dog to Lord Emms. The wretched animal, a mongrel, could not be sold for a large sum of money and, having looked after her ailing brother for a number of years, she had no intention of ministering to one of his pets. Once in the household of Lord Emms, Fido had been indulged in every way. And although passing from his first home to his second had altered the emotional pressure of Fido's environment so swiftly and to such a degree that he almost got the bends, at least he had found each master in his own way to be consistent. With the Davieses, in whose care he now found himself, this was not the case. In a single night their attitude had changed from contempt to its very opposite. Fido was relieved, but suspicious.

Obsequiousness never leads to friendship—seldom even to trust. It causes the recipient, even if he is fortified by a monstrous ego, to doubt not only those who fawn upon him but also himself. What, he wonders, can be wrong with his image that people assume he can be beguiled by such crude flattery. Fido was an intelligent animal. He quickly learned that wealth bestows only one legitimate reward: it frees the possessor from ever having to be nice to anyone.

From alertness the dog rapidly graduated to cunning.

Fido disliked Davies but, because they were both creatures of habit, he accepted him. With Mrs. Davies he responded to the fitful bouts of affection but was dismayed that, when her husband was present, she ignored him. This made the dog regard her as unreliable. So it was she that he began to torment.

When the slightest thing displeased Fido he did not hesitate to show his annoyance. If, for instance, he was offered the leavings from the Davieses' plates, he refused to eat them and frequently succeeded in overturning his bowl with his nose. If they ignored this veiled command for a better dinner, he would arch his back and emit hideous retching sounds. Predictably, this threw the Davieses into a panic lest he be genuinely ill, and he was immediately given some lightly stewed steak. If he was not allowed the run of the entire house, he would wait until they were in bed and then prowl up and down the long hall slapping his claws on the marble floor or he would pound the door of the room to which he had been confined until the sound was like thunder. Only when taken for a walk did he abandon these tantrums and display his former sunny disposition. This change of mood was most noticeable when he was among sheep. He was delighted by the perturbation that his sorties caused among his woolly friends, and this was doubled when he became aware of the positive terror that he evoked in Davies. He had no intention of running away. He knew too well on which side his biscuits were buttered, but he saw no reason not to frisk about the field behind the Great House with Davies panting after him and hissing his name for fear that shouting it would bring a farmer on the scene to quell the riot.

These escapades were so far the most disturbing manifestation of the dog's power over his guardians. The farmer who owned the land at the back of Lord Emms' house was in fact Lady Emms' nephew. The family had never approved of Agnes's disastrous marriage. They were a closely knit and very practical clan, and they did not think that having a title in the family was worth a settlement that could have been used to purchase half a county. In any case why, they asked one another, should they be in such a mad rush to marry off a relative who, as a spinster, could perform without pay any number of dreary chores about the farm. An armed neutrality had for years been maintained between the farm and the Great House, but Davies knew that if any member of that family saw Fido at his new pastime, he would be shot. In such an event, life as the Davieses were beginning to know it would cease abruptly.

After the second instance of this canine naughtiness, Fido was no longer allowed in the back garden. He scratched the side door until he broke a panel, but his jailers remained firm. They placed in front of the aperture a huge fireguard that had once been used in the nursery but which for many years now had been relegated to the attic.

Mr. Minguillan's next visit was awaited with the same terror that he always inspired, but also with eagerness. He alone could approve (and pay for) the fortifications necessary for Fido's safety. The lawyer agreed to all Davies' suggestions with an alacrity that was surprising, for the expenditure would be considerable. At either side of the garden the brick walls were tall enough to prevent any prisoner's escape, but at the back only a scraggly hedge separated Lord Emms' domain from the entire countryside beyond. It was decided that a high fence with wire netting at the top should be erected there between the row of thorn bushes and the small stream beyond. Although at one side of the garden there was a low bridge, Davies in a panic argued that there was no need for a gate in the fence that would give access to it. It seemed to him not so much an added expense but a wanton risk. Some fool might leave it open. The contractor decided otherwise, not because he had more faith in human carefulness but in order to add to the cost of the proposed work. The front garden, on the other hand, simply was not capable of being made dogproof. The delivery boys could never be relied upon to close the heavy iron gates and, in any case, from the inside the walls on either side were almost nonexistent. Therefore a piece of wire netting was added to the height of the gate by the scullery door, and on the other side of the house the pergola was strengthened and provided with a gate. The embroidery look became lost in a conglomeration of several different kinds of wood and iron and wire netting. From now onward Fido would be unable to pass from the back garden to the front without human aid. Until these improvements were complete, it was agreed that he should be taken out for his walks into the town only through the massive front gates and only at night.

Thus it came about that Davies met Raina.

Raina

Raina was a prostitute by vocation. To her, sex was the means by which she would show the world just how vile it was. In her native village she had done business with all comers, including the local policeman. By the time the neighbors had summoned up enough indignation to demand her banishment, she had summoned up enough cash to leave. Today, of course, she would have hitchhiked and possibly ended her journey richer than she started, but then the only thing for her to do was to go to the railroad station, push her entire capital through the ticket window, and ask how far it would take her. The clerk looked too tired to be tempted into any form of barter.

"Single?" he asked.

"Are you going to propose?" This riposte left the clerk looking even more tired than before, but Raina was almost bent double by a spasm of merriment. When she recovered, she was given twopence change and a ticket to Ravenage. Being a cathedral city, the place suited her needs perfectly, because even greater than her wish to make money was her desire to shock.

For this purpose she had built up a formidable armory. Her cosmetics were applied so lavishly that where her mascara ended her lipstick began. In the street she seemed to be wickedly blond because she pinned to the inside of her sequined cap two long hairpieces which hung down on either side of her face like sheets of gilded corrugated iron. Indoors her hair was

as short as a boy's and was rich mouse in color. At work she wore what was at that time the regulation costume for her profession —a frilly satin blouse, a wraparound skirt, black stockings, and glacé kid shoes with heels so high that she could never quite straighten her knees.

If she looked even odder than she intended, it was because most of these garments had been bought by post. When Davies first spoke to her, the evenings were still very cold. Her bare arms were covered by what seemed to be a large rug of black fur. This was a present from a client whom she had met the first evening she arrived in Ravenage and with whom, breaking one of her golden rules, she was becoming friendly. She had already reconnoitered the terrain and would have liked to use the square in front of the cathedral as her beat, but a few steps over the rough cobblestones there had proved this to be impossible. She settled for the junction of the main road and the nice quiet street that led to Lord Emms' house.

Experience had long since taught her the folly of carrying a handbag. As a simple country girl she had once gone into a dark doorway with two youths. There she had passed her bag to one of the young men while she employed both hands to fulfill the inordinate requirements of his friend. At the critical moment the boy who was only a spectator ran off with the evening's takings. Now, she carried only her keys at work, and it was the faint playful tinkling of these that Fido heard as he sauntered by. He gave a courteous bark.

"Hallo, handsome," Raina drawled.

Davies was immediately excited by this greeting and readily allowed the dog to lead him toward the shop entrance in which the woman was standing. He had seen her once before but, because he had been with his wife, he had not so much as turned his eyes in her direction. Even if he had been alone he would never have dared to speak. Now, by a miracle, the groundwork was being laid for him. If anything occurred that frightened him, he could blame the dog and retreat without loss of face.

Fido was beset by no such doubts. He thrust his nose up Raina's skirt and, when she squawked with laughter, wagged his tail. The formalities over, the three of them strolled along the pavement. A spaniel passing on the opposite side of the road formed the opinion that Fido was getting too big for his collar but, for once, Davies was delighted with the dog's behavior.

When they reached the house where the woman lived, she asked almost indifferently, "Do you want to come up?"

Davies did not reply, but he continued to stand in front of her. She explained her tariff and how much each item would cost. Some of the items seemed to be in a language her customer did not understand. By the time she had completed her description of this extremely varied menu, she had opened her front door. Fido looked inside the hall with eager curiosity.

"Anything at all," said Davies, bewildered and blushing.

Laughing softly for once, Raina led her guests up the stairs. "You make me die," she said. "You really do." A lot of men she knew were nervous, even embarrassed, but this extraordinary little runt was polite.

Although she referred to her home as a flat, Raina was really never going to own anything so grand. She lived in two rooms on the second floor of a building so narrow that from the front it looked as though it were a juvenile delinquent being taken into custody by the houses on either side. Every time she went out she had to lock both rooms; it was inconvenient, but the premises were cheap. Double doors connected the two halves of her kingdom but a huge mahogany wardrobe had been placed in front of them so that clients would not be apprehensive about unwarranted intrusion.

Raina led her guests into the front room. This initial visit took place at about seven o'clock on a wintry evening, but even if it had been high noon the place would still have seemed twilit. The window was at all times shrouded in Nottingham lace. The first thing the hostess did was to draw yet another curtain—this time of crimson plush.

"Turn up the gas, ducky," she said. "It's by the fireplace." She had decided that it would be amusing, when addressing this funny little man, to decorate her discourse with terms of endearment. They contrasted so ludicrously with his timid formality.

When the light was increased, the full luxury of the setting was revealed. Most of the room was occupied by a brass bed. On this lay an artificial-silk counterpane, a mountain of brocaded, braided, tasseled cushions that she herself had cobbled up, and a doll in some kind of national costume. Here and there around the room were improvised still lifes that would have delighted the hearts of the Pre-Raphaelites. Her dressing table was loaded with toilet accessories— a painted hairbrush, a comb with a metal back, even a shoehorn, and any number of whisky- and rum-colored perfumes which had obviously been selected not for their scent but because the shapes of their bottles were so bizarre. Nearby was an octagonal table covered with a Spanish shawl on which stood a vase containing paper flowers the size of cabbages, a photograph of her nude self, and a string of amber beads which had not been left there by accident.

Fido padded about the floor, his nose flinching at the exotic smells, to which was immediately added the scent of incense. His master, if such he could be called, lowered himself cautiously into an armchair and, with bulging eyes, absorbed his first glimpse of sin. Raina drew the cover from the bed like a conjuror so as to leave the cushions and the doll almost un-moved; then more slowly she stripped herself, pausing from time to time to strike a bawdy attitude.

Her body was as thin as an excuse and a silvery white all over. Even her knees showed no sign of being nourished by her circulation. It was as though a birch tree had seen its error halfway through the process of taking human form. When she was naked she put on her shoes again and, sliding onto the bed, beckoned to her guest to join her.

Mr. Davies undressed as much as he did to take his

habitual afternoon nap, and lay down beside her. He was trembling from head to foot but nothing happened.

Raina turned onto her side and made painstaking efforts to discover in Braille what her customer wanted. He facilitated her inquiries but nothing happened.

She heaved herself higher up on the cushions and asked if he felt all right. "Because I don't want you dying in my flat," she added, so as not on any account to seem sympathetic. Mr. Davies assured her that he was enjoying his visit greatly but still nothing happened. Raina lit a cigarette and began to talk shop. This, she had found, sometimes roused a sluggish customer. Her lurid tales were interwoven with passages of misanthropic philosophy and punctuated with shrieks of mirthless laughter. She had positions but no magnitude; opinions but no thoughts; starkly undefended preferences but no taste. What saved her discourse from banality was her astonishing self-awareness. "I know they're not interested in me. I say to them, 'If you don't like my face, put a cushion over it.'" Mr. Davies could have listened for a thousand and one nights but still nothing happened.

After about half an hour as Scheherazade's understudy, Raina became aware that she was cold. She was getting restless. So was Fido. He was bored with lying in front of a gas fire, which had gone out, and had begun to pace the room. He even gave an experimental bark.

"Shut up," shouted Raina in a voice much louder than the noise against which she was protesting. The dog, no longer willing to be addressed in this manner, barked again.

"Tell him to stop that," Raina demanded, turning to her bedfellow.

Davies got up and, stroking the dog's head, asked him with the utmost politeness to be quiet. Fido's answer was to utter a slightly smaller sound; he did not want it thought that he was anyone's dumb friend.

"He likes you," said Davies, looking sideways at Raina.

Wrongly construing this remark to be conciliatory, she ignored it. The weird session seemed to be at an end. "It'll still cost you two pounds," she said when her client was fully dressed.

"Yes, of course." Davies proffered the money. "It's been a most enjoyable evening. I hope we meet again soon."

"Tomorrow, if you've got the cash."

At the door of her room, as he fastened Fido's chain to his collar, Davies again said, "He's interested in you." He tittered uncertainly.

Raina patted the dog's head perfunctorily. "Randy beast," she called after him as he descended the stairs.

On the way home, Davies, for the first time, chatted with Fido. He thought that he foresaw a day when, instead of fighting over who was the master and who the slave, they might become, if not friends, confederates.

"Where have you been?" Mrs. Davies demanded when they returned home. The words were less a question than a rebuke. She addressed them to Fido; it avoided a direct confrontation. But as the remark was not aimed at him, Davies saw no reason to reply.

The Davieses' marriage had always been largely silent. In the beginning Mrs. Davies had not minded that she was bad at expressing herself. In times of trouble (and they were many), she had only to stand beside her husband to feel at the least a little reassured. The very poor try to borrow from the poor; they are ashamed, impotent, in the presence of the rich, who they rightly think will not be able to sympathize with their predicament. On the same principle, Mrs. Davies was glad that her husband was weak and small, because then it did not put her to shame if he saw that she was afraid. But as time passed, the tide of jeopardy receded. Their dependence on one another grew less. Nothing then stuck out of the water so sharply as the rocks of their dissimilarities. If they were alive today, they would wear each other's clothes, share each other's views, interchange their domestic functions, but then the barriers between the sexes were impassable; they could not concur in even the most trivial issues. Man had appetites; women had emotions. The only way in which a marriage could be made to work was for each party to forgive the other for being of the opposite sex.

Davies was not prepared to sink as low as this. As, in his own estimation, he became more like his social superiors, aping their manners, adopting their speech patterns, reading the same newspaper, he more and more deeply despised his wife for remaining primitively emotional in middle life. This was a time when he thought that sentimentality should be replaced by that common sense which he identified with coldness. And so the silence of their marriage had degenerated from a conspiracy of stubbornness to a mere convenience. It saved her the bother of trying to express her unformed yearnings, while he was spared all attempts to explain the world to her.

Now their relationship was changing yet again. She could not stop herself from hoping that some drop of joy could be distilled from Lord Emms' death. Her husband, on the other hand, refused to be openly happy. It would be undignified, immature. Tonight he retreated even further into his distant dreams because for the first time, he thought, they might be capable of fulfillment.

The only events that did anything to unite the Davieses was the prospect of Mr. Minguillan's regular invasions of the Great House, a prospect they both hated. These visits were to be more or less monthly occurrences, but it was not certain that they would take place on the same day of each month. Mrs. Davies asked, in the most subservient voice, when she might expect the lawyer's next call but, though he smiled, he did not reply. Except for his name, which he spelled out for them, they learned nothing about him.

Mr. Minguillan
Returns

His first visit had been enlivened by discussion of the arrangements for the fences; the second started with the vigorous testing of them. Mr. Minguillan locked and unlocked each gate several times and swung them all back and forth; he also shook the fences until Mrs. Davies became quite nervous. Inside the house it became obvious that the procedure was always going to be monotonously the same. When he was already halfway up the stairs, he asked if he might inspect the rooms. His solemn perambulations complete, he sat at the dining-room table to receive a cup of coffee and to have an audience with Fido.

This farcical part of the ritual made the Davieses very uneasy. Mrs. Davies did not sit during the interrogation despite its length. Quite seriously, Mr. Minguillan took the animal's head in his hands and staring into his eyes asked, "Are you happy? Are you being well looked after?" The dog wagged its tail. Then the lawyer turned a less concentrated attention on the servants. "Everything seems most satisfactory. Are there any problems?" At this the first encounter, Davies had said that they had met with no difficulties. He only longed to get the intruder out of the house as quickly as possible. The Davieses' fears were nameless, but this man's presence disturbed them deeply. He was so dark and so big and his weight must have been doubled by his eyebrows, which clung fiercely, like black gorse, to the cliffs overhanging his cavernous eyes.

The more the humans disliked Mr. Minguillan, the more the dog approved. He liked his harsh, astringent smell, so different from the oily odor of the Davieses. As a compliment he slobbered a little on the crotch of the lawyer's floppy but immaculate suit.

By the time the second interview came around, Davies decided that it had been foolish to focus all his ingenuity on trying to cut the interview short. He felt it must be possible to make use of the lawyer in some way. He primed his wife to say that everything in the shops was becoming dearer. This ruse was a mistake. It led Mr. Minguillan to ask that in future he might be given an itemized list of everything spent on the dog or the house with the appropriate receipts. In subsequent months it was only when, with his huge pale lips moving faintly, he had read every word of this catalogue that he handed over any money. During his tour of the grounds he had noticed the overgrown kitchen garden. He suggested that, as spring was approaching, Davies should grow his own vegetables. This, he pointed out, would lessen the bills.

Though the Davieses' life was to become a series of invasions by Mr. Minguillan for which they prepared and from which they recovered, it was just as well that he watched over them so keenly. His visits gave Mrs. Davies the pattern for living, an occupation for her hands, without which she might have lost completely her already frail hold on reality. Had it not been for the quirky nature of Lord Emms' will, what would have become of her? The paltry wages that she had been paid for the past twenty-five years had permitted her to accumulate only the most meager savings, which would never allow her to retire; and then, she was too young to go into a home for the aged and too old to find new employment.

The house was big enough for her to "do" roughly a room a day between one of the lawyer's visits and the next. Through the winter she occasionally lighted a small fire in one of the bedrooms to prevent it from becoming damp. If she was alone in the house, she sat on the edge of her ladyship's bed for a while or stood by the window in one of the guest rooms. From habit, she never felt at home anywhere but in her own room or the kitchen. She lingered in other parts of the house more to justify the futile care she took of the place than for any other reason.

She gazed out onto the garden that Davies was allowing to go to seed and watched the last few birds lance with their sudden beaks the blue-green lawn. It was what to herself she always called a "bad time of year." The coldest days might be still to come. Her mind drifted toward the memory of Christmas as it was in years gone by. It had been a season when the usually rigid protocol of the servants' quarters was relaxed a little. The ancient butler had danced with her even when she was only the kitchen maid. It had been an excruciatingly embarrassing experience, but it was something to look back on. Now that whole way of life was being swept away and nothing that she was able to understand had come to take its place. Even people seemed to have changed.

It was almost impossible for the Davieses to make friends. Their training had made them painfully aware of their exact station in life. They had learned how to bow before their betters and how to condescend to their inferiors but, in the presence of their equals, they had very little idea of what to do. They had been given so little practice. At the time when these social habits were formed, there had been no houses as grand as theirs in Ravenage. But Lord Emms gave no parties; no coachmen were given beer in the kitchen; no house guests were entertained; no lady's maids came to stay.

Before their employer died, the Davieses had on occasion gone to a public house but they could not rid themselves of the notion that they were slumming, and it showed. Now excursions into the town were even more embarrassing than before. They found that they had become objects of undisguised curiosity. Lord Emms' funeral had caused quite a stir precisely because it caused so little. In the neighborhood, estimates of his wealth were greatly exaggerated, and it seemed odd to the townfolk that such a rich man's burial should flush out only four mourners, two of whom were his servants. Then, when it became known that the Davieses were to stay on in the Great House, inquisitiveness could not be restrained. It was the opinion of the butcher's boy that they were waiting to become the housekeepers of another tenant. The milkman thought they would be leaving shortly, while the postman spread it abroad that they would be wealthy as soon as their employer's will was probated.

One morning, as Mrs. Davies was standing beside her husband in the newspaper shop, the girl who was not bothering to serve anybody said, "Sad about the old fellow, wasn't it?" Mrs. Davies smiled wanly but did not speak. She hoped that the interrogation would end there. It did not. The next question was, "You'll be staying on for a while, will you?"

"I expect so."

"It's a lovely place."

"We've always tried to keep it nice."

At the other end of the counter a couple were watching and shamelessly listening to this dialogue. The man asked his companion a question, of which nothing was audible but the final word, "rich." The woman replied, "They haven't exactly blossomed out, have they?"

This the Davieses heard all too clearly; they also heard the laughter that followed it.

Mrs. Davies
and
Mrs. Adie

Unlike her husband, Mrs. Davies felt her loneliness keenly. She had no inner life. Although she sometimes read the easier passages of the newspapers, she now felt it was pointless to immerse herself in those works by Annie Swann that she had so much enjoyed when she was a parlor maid. Over the years her imagination had died of starvation. She could still respond to natural things; she could breathe in the forlorn air of the garden at dusk; she could watch the dance of the firelight around the bedroom walls. But, like some small children, she could not entertain herself.

In this and in many other ways of which she was unaware, she resembled Fido. Though she had been a party to an attempt on his life, she was prepared to let bygones be bygones and be his friend, but there were difficulties. One of these was that it was too cold to play in the garden and the little indoor games that they had invented for themseleves he now played so boisterously that she feared some precious china ornament might be broken or some delicate piece of furniture become scratched. When this seemed likely, Mrs. Davies grew hysterically apprehensive. If she could, she slipped into the nearest room and shut herself in. The dog would scratch the door violently for a few minutes and then slink off to the kitchen. She had good reason to dread the thought of any damage occurring to his lordship's valuable possessions. Such an accident would not pass unnoticed for long. Mr. Minguillan had taken an inventory of everything in the house. If there was a breakage, Mrs. Davies feared that, as in times gone by, the cost of repairs would be deducted from her wages.

She knew the dog tormented her deliberately, but the nightmare of what would happen if he died worried her even more. When she mentioned this aspect of their situation to her husband, he flatly refused to contemplate their future. "He's hardly full-grown," he protested. "A fine dog like that, with the way we look after him, might live for twelve years or more. It's no good looking further ahead than that." It did not occur to Mrs. Davies that secretly he might be even more worried than she.

As far as Mrs. Davies knew, which was a very short distance indeed, her husband had her interests at heart at least when they coincided with his own. Even though their relationship had deteriorated noticeably in the last few weeks, she did not think of him as disloyal, but he never displayed any compassion for her vague doubts, her undirected yearnings. The only person who in any measure fulfilled this function was a certain Mrs. Adie. She was housekeeper to the bishop of Ravenage. Some years before, the two women had been waiting side by side in Alton's—the bake shop that sold the cakes her ladyship had liked so much—and Mrs. Davies had recognized at once that the stranger was standing on the same rung of the social ladder as she. Her manners were so much better than those of the upper class and her clothes were so much worse. Even so, Mrs. Davies would never have spoken first. It was Mrs. Adie

who said, "You're from the big house, aren't you?" Mrs. Davies
had nodded demurely. At a first meeting this was as far as she
would go toward a public statement about herself.

After this initial encounter there followed months of nodding on busy days and, when there was time to spare, polite
phrases uttered while looking into shop windows. Then Mrs.
Adie invited her acquaintance to what she called "a little supper." The next week, Mrs. Davies offered a return of hospitality
to show that she knew how to go on. For a while they raced
cutlet for cutlet toward greater intimacy, but the evenings
spent in Lord Emms' house were never as nice. While the
master was alive, time off for the staff was only theoretical. He
was always ringing the bell or even invading their part of the
house to ask for something he could perfectly easily have
found for himself. The bishop never did anything like that.
Mrs. Adie had a cozy little room of her own with an upholstered chair. At Lord Emms' house Mr. Davies was usually
sitting around. Sometimes he pointedly read the paper and
refused to take part in the conversation even when the guest
politely tried to draw him in; on other occasions, provoked by
something foolish that one of the women had said, he delivered a long lecture on the evils of modern life. For these
reasons, and despite her strong sense of social obligation, Mrs.
Davies found that it was more often she who was the guest and
her friend the hostess.

In a group of women, whether of two or two hundred,
there is almost always a different atmosphere from that which

prevails if even only one man is present—even such an apparently sexless being as Davies. It is more relaxed, softer, more basic and natural as opposed to merely cynical. In this world of wall-to-wall femininity Mrs. Davies felt more at home than anywhere else. She distrusted—often did not understand—the flirtatious wit that fills the air in mixed company and, though she occasionally spoke badly of people, she never indulged in the stylized cattiness that women seem to think makes them attractive to men. She did not refrain from these social pastimes on principle but by nature. Therefore to her the spurious charitableness of Mrs. Adie seemed sincere. In reality it was protective coloring drawn from the household in which she worked. St. Theresa said that we should treat all people as though they were better than ourselves. It will be noted that she did not say they actually were better. How saintly can you get? The bishop used the same method. Through the years he had worked out a technique of behavior and, more particularly, a mode of speech that completely masked his assurance of his moral superiority. Sometimes his housekeeper followed his example so closely that she quoted his actual phrases. Mrs. Davies mistook this catalogue of bland axioms for real generosity of spirit. Consequently she felt closer to her friend than the difference between their characters warranted.

In modern life, Mrs. Davies could have discussed without immodesty such a subject as the failure—nay, the disappearance—of her sex life with Davies. By our standards, the conversation which these two ladies thought intimate would seem formal, even distant. They complained to each other about the price of goods in the shops but never spoke of their wages. If Mrs. Davies had tried to mention such a subject, her friend would undoubtedly have led her away from it. This she would have done not because she wasn't curious but because she could remember an occasion when one of the bishop's daughters had said to him that their neighbor had no money to speak of. His grace had looked pained and replied, "But money is never to speak of."

All these evidences of refinement in her friend made it impossible for Mrs. Davies ever to mention her real worries. Most of all was it impossible to say that she and her husband, in a sense, were now employed by a dog and that she hated it.

In spite of these tacit restraints, she spent many peaceful, even happy, evenings at the bishop's palace. Usually the conversation meandered among the foothills of metaphysics; it was about life. The fact that Mrs. Davies spoke in Christmas-card language annoyed her husband. He felt she was insincere, but he was wrong. She also thought in platitudes. To her, time did fly; she did find folk strange; her world was small. Mrs. Adie listened without criticizing her companion's sentiments or expressions but offered counter-axioms drawn from Christian doctrine. In these Mrs. Davies neither believed nor disbelieved. She hadn't the intellectual muscle for such a decision. Like a child she sucked on her friend's apparent solicitude, her comfort, her patience. It was the cupboard love of the soul. Without it she would have truly starved.

Fido and
Raina

On the face of it, Mr. Davies had just as much cause to feel frustrated as his wife, but he did not doubt and he did not yearn. Instead he quarreled with her, railed against the world, and cursed the dog—though, to avoid rousing the animal's anger, this he did in a soft, cooing voice. People who know a great many words never suffer at all, except physically. Even men like Davies with a limited vocabulary can extract from it some relief from their rage and grief. He was also helped by having a rich, even turgid imagination. In it he tidied up the social disorder created by contemporary politicians, priests, and reformers or, without acknowledging any contradiction, indulged in some very unruly sexual fantasies. So far all his life he had accepted easily, perhaps gladly the impossibility of realizing his secret desires. His straitened circumstances and his lack of physical endowments, in a sense, had saved him from himself. But that was before he met Raina.

Now he was safe no more, and this knowledge was both dreadful and exciting.

When he was not with her, he despised her. She was common and her ideas were predictable without being logical, but when he sat in her gaudy room and listened to her gaudy tales, he was fascinated. She regarded him as a caution; she mocked him, but she didn't judge him. He was by no means the first of her customers who was entertained more by words than by actions, but unlike any of the others, Mr. Davies never uttered a single obscene phrase. Sometimes she would pick out one of her favorite words and shout, "Say it. Go on, say it." Her guest would lower his paper-thin eyelids and simper but no coarse sound would issue from his pursed lips. After watching his face closely for a second, Raina would shriek with mocking laughter and throw her silvery legs in the air like a corpse getting the stiffness out of its limbs.

It was inevitable that, after a few evenings spent lying by the fire, the dog would get onto the bed with this ill-sorted couple.

Fido was a hard-line Darwinian. If his detractors (and among dogs of high degree he had many) had known this, they would have called him a zoological climber. As it was, they merely thought he had ideas above his pedigree. Originally this had been true. He had come from a good home but, when he was bequeathed to Lord Emms, he was not slow to realize that he had improved himself. Not only were his surroundings more luxurious, the carpets softer to his belly, and the food tastier, but greater attention was paid to him. At that time, if there had been such a thing as a self-made thoroughbred, that is what he would have wished to become. With the sudden, unexplained departure of his second master, he had, for a few days, been confused. Then his confidence had been restored. Indeed it had increased. In puppyhood, he had been treated with affection; in adolescence he received reverence. This caused a radical change in the nature of his ambitions. He ceased as a matter of policy to ignore all other mongrels; he started to ignore all dogs.

When animals born in captivity are introduced to members of their own species, they frequently refuse to form even momentary attachments to them. They long ago fell in love with their keepers when these persons were the only living beings they ever saw. As far as he knew, Fido was an only puppy. His life had always consisted of hours of languid daydreams alternating with periods of boredom. When tedium overtook him, he demanded entertainment from the humans around him. As time went by, these requests passed from being winsome to being insistent.

If anything, such as a pair of slippers put before the fire to dry, prevented him from lying comfortably on the kitchen hearth rug, he went into another room and sat barking in front of the empty grate. When Mrs. Davies, rather than light a separate fire for him, tried to drag him away, he growled at her ominously. He no longer stood around waiting with uplifted head for his meals. Instead he put his paws on the drainboard where his steak was being cut up and snatched pieces of meat, which he ate raw.

To a greater and greater degree he was taking his life into his own paws. If he was involved in any kind of argument with people, he found a way of stating his case clearly. If he played games, he did not want exercise; he wanted victory.

It was almost inevitable that he should grow up in this way. If a person considers himself underprivileged and envies a group of people whom he thinks better off than he, given the slightest opportunity, he will imitate the worst characteristics of that group. Fido's one desire was to become as horrible as a human being, and through Davies and Raina he was to be granted his wish.

During all these strange meetings with her client, the woman had accepted mild displays of affection from the dog with the minimum of reciprocation. Not until he jumped on the bed and lay down beside her did she give him for the first time her whole attention. She had never thought that she ought to conceal her indifference out of politeness to its owner, since the man himself took so little notice of the animal. Now, to her surprise, he leaned across her naked body and stroked the dog slowly from head to tail. "He's really fond of you," he said for the hundredth time. With these words he slithered off the bed like a master of ceremomies leaving the stage to a star. At last it dawned on Raina to what climax all these evenings had been a prelude. In a flash of intuition she saw that the odd behavior of this little gnome was not due to his shyness but to his obliquity. What she could not understand, because she knew so little of his past, was that the soul of Mr. Davies had become captive to his way of living. He had long ago lost all capacity for direct enjoyment. His destiny was to assist at the feasts of others.

Revulsion caused Raina's flesh to creep over her birdlike bones. "This," she said, "is really going to cost you."

None of the participants in this scene thought that what they were doing was a sin. Sin is an idea that has to be redefined by each god as he is voted into power. What they were doing was not even a vice, though Davies may have wished it were. A vice is any habit in which the addict persists in spite of knowing that it is injurious to his well-being. Fido felt that he was fulfilling an aspiration, and Davies, who would have drunk champagne through a straw, guessed that the evening's entertainment, although utterly oblique, was the only kind of pleasure he was ever going to know. Raina did what she did for money. All her actions were therefore sacred.

It had taken only a few visits to Leman Street, spread over a fortnight, for their true purpose to emerge. Once the private pattern was established, there seemed no change to the neighbors. Raina would never allow one client to call on her incessantly or at the same time on the same day of the week. She hated inevitability, preferring an endless chain of partners dancing to different tunes. Through all vicissitudes of fortune, she remained her languid, wayward self. Nothing about her changed except her price.

The financial variability of their relationship would once have kept Davies in check but lately his disposition had changed. A short time ago he could not have brought himself to address Raina at all. Now, if failing to find her at home, he and Fido met her on the street corner; he not only spoke to her, he importuned her—though always in the most genteel manner. What had not altered and would always inhibit him was his inability to do anything precipitately even to procure his own pleasure. He habitually cleared his throat and took a deep breath before saying anything deliciously unkind to his wife; before he ate the food on his plate he moved it about with his fork. He approached the hours he spent in Leman Street with the same preparation. They were so exciting that he would not have had the nervous stamina to survive a rapid succession of them. In any case, his sense of propriety would have been outraged by a debauch.

Only the dog saw no need for restraint. Until now he had been fractious only at home. His slaves supposed that the house and garden had begun to bore him. Out of doors it had occasionally been difficult to coax him past a particularly interesting tree trunk or lamppost, but otherwise his deportment had been exemplary.

Suddenly on his evening walks he quite brazenly dragged his companion down the street of his capricious choice. As often as not, their erratic course ended up outside the house where Raina lived. If the front door was not already open, Fido would back into the road until he could easily look up at the second-floor window; then he began to bark. At this the landlord, who lived at the ground-floor front and who was by nature part jailer and part pimp, would draw back from his window a wisp of gray net and either shake his head from side to side with his features bent into a tragic mask or up and down with twinkling eyes and bared teeth. Davies, who had hoped that his visits to this house of ill-repute would forever pass unnoticed, hated both these pieces of mime, but Fido was proud to have learned the language so quickly. If the signs were negative, he immediately started to pull Davies back the way they had come; if they were good, he pounded the door with his feet. The occupants of the houses opposite watched this performance with indignation or amusement depending upon whether or not they found it shocking.

If, as she was fond of declaring to her husband, Mrs. Davies really did not have a single friend in the world, she might have been spared the appearance of yet another cloud across her already somber sky. She might never have known that Davies was in the habit of visiting the house of a notorious prostitute. Who can bring such unsettling news as this to any woman except her bosom companion?

Naturally it was not at the house of the late Lord Emms that this scandal was related. There the anti-hero of Mrs. Adie's saga might have crept into the room while his name was on her lips. It was at the bishop's palace, in the little room with the upholstered chair, that the hostess, altering her tone of voice slightly, asked her guest the apparently innocuous question, "Is your husband well?"

"He keeps well enough, thank you," Mrs. Davies replied. "He's a good man but moody. I expect they all are."

"Does he take plenty of exercise?"

"More than ever he used to. It's the dog, you see."

"I've heard he's been seen a lot in the town with that dog."

"Heard?" Already Mrs. Davies was uneasy. "I suppose with a dog that size, he's bound to be noticed . . . It's such a light color," she sighed as she recalled this added affront to respectability.

"He's been seen a lot in Leman Street." Before she could

bring herself to say this, Mrs. Adie felt compelled to turn away from her guest. She moved the lamp a few inches along the gleaming tablecloth.

"Leman Street." Mrs. Davies repeated the words in complete bewilderment.

"I don't wonder you don't know the place. I don't expect you've ever even walked through it."

"I don't think I have."

"Exactly."

"Exactly what?"

"It has a very bad name—at least one house in it has."

"You mean . . . You're trying to tell me that Davies has been to that house?" In her agitation she forgot to refer to him as "Mr."

"Yes."

"No." Mrs. Davies put down her cup hastily as though it were the tea that was too bitter to swallow. She remembered to thank her hostess for telling her what she would rather not have known. Then, putting on her galoshes, she made excuses for her sudden departure and stepped out into the damp night.

Arriving home, she found the house in darkness. She stomped about the kitchen, of two minds about whether or not to make any supper at all for her husband but habit was too strong. Her hands prepared a meal automatically while her mind fluttered about the room like a frantic moth, trying to settle upon a solution to her unprecedented problem. It was not the unfaithfulness that she wished she could undo; it was the scandal. If she could find no way of forcing Davies to give up his visits to this street of shame, it would soon not only be in the newspaper shop that she was talked about. In the streets and in places where till now she had always been respected she would become a figure of fun. When she imagined the look the assistant in Alton's would give her, she could not refrain from shedding a few tears. As soon as she heard her husband coming up the drive in conversation with the dog, she started up the stairs. She could not face him yet. "I'm going to bed," she shouted in a shaky voice. "Your supper's on the stove."

"What's got into her?" Davies asked the dog.

All next day, Mrs. Davies kept out of her husband's way by spring-cleaning one of the upper rooms. She kept hoping that onto her lips would fall the words that would make him see how conspicuous he had become. But no miraculous gift of tongues was bestowed upon her. After supper, worn out with work and anxiety, she could no longer bother to sit in another room. When, with studied reluctance, Davies said that he supposed he must take the dog for a walk, his wife, who had never before made any comment upon this almost nightly remark, asked why.

"What do you mean 'Why'?"

"Why can't he just go out into the garden? He can't come to any harm, not with all those doors and fences and everything."

Davies considered this suggestion with a calmness that surprised his wife. Last time he had called at Leman Street a man whom he had not previously seen had come to the door and announced that Raina was ill. "Oh, I see," Mr. Davies had said. He could think of only one illness in connection with a prostitute, and he was worried. The stranger was evidently a mind reader, for he hastily explained that Raina's stomach was upset. He laid one white hand on the midriff of his almost skintight suit as though he were going to do a South American dance. "Give it a few days," he suggested. Because of this conversation and because, incidentally, it was raining, it suited Davies to pander to his wife's strange new mood. Leading the dog cautiously by his gold collar, he opened the scullery door and, before the animal realized what was happening, he was outside.

As soon as Fido discovered that he was the victim of a heartless hoax, he clawed at the back door until it seemed that the little glass panels would fall out. Mrs. Davies put her elbows on the table and her hands over her ears. When this bombardment proved ineffectual, the dog tried to jump the gate at the side of the house. The piece of wire netting that had been added at the top made it too high for even Fido to clear. He hurt himself slightly in the attempt, which added to his sense of outrage. Angrier than ever, he ran around to the arbor at the back of the house. Instinct warned him not to break the French windows, so he settled for leaning against them for shelter from the driving rain. There he stood wailing until Mrs. Davies lost her nerve and let him in.

In the kitchen Mrs. Davies found a towel with which to dry

his back. For this operation he put his large forepaws on her knees. She asked him who was a bad boy but could not resist laying her cheek against his bowed head. They sustained this affecting tableau until she became aware of a warm, moist feeling round her ankles.

She jumped up and stared down at the small pool of liquid that lay at her feet.

"Wicked, wicked boy," she growled in an effort to sound threatening. Fido remained unrepentant. He even gave his tail an arrogant wag. When Mrs. Davies tried to whip him with the towel, he darted out of the room to look for a good place in which to perpetrate an even grosser act of defilement. He had suddenly discovered that he possessed two extra weapons for use against his jailers. They were almost as effective as his teeth and claws, and they could be brought into play with far less effort. He felt proud of himself. He had transcended a convention which humans had imposed upon him almost from birth for their own squeamish convenience.

Enter
Mr. Sylvester

The man who had answered the doorbell at the notorious house in Leman Street was called Mr. Sylvester. Raina had met him the day after her arrival in Ravenage. She had wandered through the center of the city, up one street and down another like a water diviner searching for indications of the existence of a hidden spring of wealth. Within minutes of her instinctive willow switch turning in her hands, this man had approached her. At their first encounter she had charged him her usual rustic prices. He had paid and asked for another appointment. This she would not grant. It was boring, she explained, to know that was going to happen next week. She pointed out that, unless she was lucky, he would find her at the same place most evenings.

Three nights later, he again accosted her at the street corner that she was beginning to make her very own. "I want to have a long chat with you," he said.

"Oh, God," Raina moaned, "not another damn talker."

"Seriously."

"That will cost you twice as much." Though the customer remained unmoved by this riposte, the girl fell against the lamppost in a paroxysm of mirth.

Back in the twilit room, she began automatically to undress until her client stopped her. "Come and sit down," he said gently. Very slowly he tried to convince her that she could earn twice the money that she was getting at present with an expenditure of half the effort by simply increasing her rural fees. Moreover, by charging more she would attract a better class of customer. "Sin," he explained, "is like perfume. If it's cheap no one will buy it."

Raina was genuinely indifferent to class. It was not her experience that gents gave any less trouble. In fact, as a rule, they took longer. It was with obvious impatience that she allowed Mr. Sylvester to proceed with his lecture on economics. Suddenly she could bear no more. "They won't know what I'm charging," she burst out. "Not until they ask me and then it will . . . Oh, for heaven's sake! All I'll do is lose the mugs I've already got."

Her mentor explained that, doing things his way, she need no longer solicit. He would find customers for her; all she would have to do was sit at home and receive them. Though this proposition did not meet with her approval, at least it aroused her suspicion. "What's in it for you?" she asked.

Mr. Sylvester replied, "I was coming to that." He was not finding it easy to win Raina over to his standard of values. His one desire in life was not to have to work and, to this end, he took what risks were necessary. This was not an outlook that could ever touch her ample spirit. She was one of nature's pirates. She did not want to remain in harbor while others, less courageous than she, took to the open seas. She enjoyed her raids along the coast of respectability. While she could still move, nothing would prevent her from walking the streets. If she had thought it would work, she would have gone from door to door in Ravenage, offering her services like a tinker.

In the end she and Mr. Sylvester reached a compromise, not because she had been convinced by the logic of his arguments, as he imagined, but because she liked him. She graciously consented to remain at home to entertain whatever customers he found for her, and he permitted her to walk up and down her beat when time allowed. After a few adjustments and a few screaming matches, this scheme worked perfectly. In fact, so totally did Raina and Mr. Sylvester find themselves in agreement that they got married.

To him the occasion was more of a merger than a sacrament. He felt that by offering her a long-term contract, he would make her feel relaxed and therefore better able to concentrate on her work. One could have described the money spent on the license as an investment except that he did not pay. The words of the ceremony implied that he would look after her if anything prevented her permanently from earning their living. As it happened, this pledge was never put to a test.

Raina would have liked to be married in the cathedral with a train and a veil. In his opposition to this proposal, her fiancé was obdurate. She gave way. Apart from wearing a new white satin blouse instead of one of her well-worn multicolored ones, she did not protest her purity.

She deferred to Mr. Sylvester in many ways. She really was taken with him, and especially with the artificiality of his appearance. His hair was parted in the middle and waved with the utmost symmetry. He had a moustache so thin that some of the way it went in single file. To keep it absolutely even, he sat before Raina's mirror and applied her eyebrow pencil to his upper lip. While he was there he polished his nails with her leather buffer. Because of these refinements, the fact that he was so slim, and the ludicrous neatness of his façade, it occurred to his wife that he might be homosexual. She did not know the word but she knew what it meant. During the many night-long discussions in which she had been involved with clients, almost everything that one person can do to another had been explained and, on occasion, demonstrated to her. On the day they were married she had asked her bridegroom if he was one of those men who usually went with boys.

The reply was, "If need be." Embroidering upon this theme, Mr. Sylvester told her that she could always recommend him if one of her customers was at all that way inclined. Nevertheless, to mark the occasion and at the same time prove his versatility, when they had drunk the bottle of champagne that she had bought, he made love to her. This he had not done since the first evening they met.

Raina was to learn, quite soon after this conversation, that none of the signs that had made her question his heterosexuality meant that he was weak. It was his idea that she should purchase the huge wardrobe that filled the space in front of the double doors connecting her rooms. She was allowed to keep in it various coats made from skins in which no animal would be (or had been) seen dead, her peignoirs of chiffon trimmed with monkey fur and of black lace threaded with pink ribbon, and

her innumerable pairs of shoes, but it was less an article of furniture than a right of way. As soon as this monumental mahogany structure was heaved into position, Mr. Sylvester set about cutting a rectangular hole in the back which could be covered by a curtain. "If it makes them feel any cozier in their minds, let them see you lock that door," he said, pointing to the one that led onto the landing. "This one," he added, holding the door of the wardrobe, "we'll fix so that it shuts tight without having to be locked. If anything goes wrong, open this or bang on it or do something that I can hear, and I'll be here in a flash." While he spoke he drew from his breast pocket a cutthroat razor, which he pretended to draw across her throat. She took in a deep breath but before she could expostulate, he added, "But never, never scream. It might bring the police."

Not many days after he had delivered these instructions, Mr. Sylvester fulfilled his promise. A burly Irishman got into conversation with Raina as she was reluctantly walking home from her beat. He told her what a lovely young woman she was; she responded to these kind words by asking for money. "You shall have every bloody penny I got on me," he replied, and this in the end she did. When they were indoors he put the sum that she had specified into a vase full of peacock feathers that stood on the mantelshelf and proceeded to enjoy what he had paid for. When the time she had allotted to him was up, he declared that she had not done all the wonderful things that she had promised, and promptly returned the money to his wallet. Raina opened the wardrobe door and, as though he were part of a conjuring trick, her husband jumped into the room. The Irishman gave way to some operatic laughter on hearing himself threatened by this willowy tailor's dummy. "Put your money back wherever it was—all of it," said Mr. Sylvester, "not just that measly bit." Instead the Irishman offered his wallet to his enemy, intending to seize the hand that foolishly reached out for it. As expected, the long fingers stretched out and were grasped—but only for a second. Raina, lurking among the cushions, was amazed. As fast as the tongue of a cobra, her husband's other hand shot out from nowhere, the razor blade flashed, and the disagreement was settled. Cursing Raina for a whore, the Irishman was let out to run down the stairs holding with one hand the bleeding wrist of the other. Mr. Sylvester went immediately into the other room to wash some pink spots from the notes.

At the beginning of their married life, Mr. Sylvester spent quite a lot of time crouching among his wife's clothes. It was not that he was greatly interested in her sexual practices; he wanted to make sure that she charged the specified amounts. "You make the money," he said. "I'll invest it." This he did principally in gambling. However, he never bothered to monitor the visits of Mr. Davies. His wife had represented him as a feeble little runt who would never be any trouble to anyone. To Fido she tactfully made no reference.

On a Lead

By the time Mr. Minguillan paid his next visit to the Great House, every room stank of disinfectant. He noticed this. His huge, furry nostrils dilated and his eyebrows moved toward each other like black badgers preparing for combat. He asked if there had been a recent illness in the house or an accident. The Davieses said no. They did not dare to tell him the nature of the disaster that was becoming an almost daily occurrence. They felt he might accuse them of not feeding Fido correctly, even though he knew that they depended utterly on the dog's continued good health.

Needless to say, in the lawyer's presence Fido behaved in an exemplary fashion. While the visitor drank his coffee, the dog watched every movement and once or twice cocked his head to one side in a manner that he thought appealing. When Mr. Minguillan left, Fido accompanied him to the door and stood whimpering and trembling as he watched him depart.

It fell to Mrs. Davies to be responsible for most of the distasteful cleaning up. Her life was becoming unbearable. The one thing that she had learned to do well and that gave her the feeling that, however humbly, she served a purpose, was to keep her environment in order. Now, to do this, she had to remember to shut every door behind her wherever she went and, in the hall, which she couldn't make dog-tight, she was obliged to keep the carpets perpetually rolled up. She hated the barren look thus given to part of her kingdom.

She knew that Fido was subjecting her to this torture because she did not want him to go for real walks in the evening, but to have let him go would be simply to exchange one agony for another. She assumed that if excursions into the town were permitted, Davies would at once make for Leman Street. In fact, because of Raina's indisposition, he would have done no such thing, but of this she had no way of knowing.

After pondering over the problem for some time, she arrived at what she thought was a solution. Why should not she and her husband both accompany the dog on its evening exercise? When this suggestion was put to Davies, he flatly refused to cooperate. "It's a waste of manpower," he pointed out. "If you, for some unknown reason, want to take him out, go."

Mrs. Davies tried this, only to find that, within a few yards of the gates, she was leaning back at an angle of forty-five degrees from the ground while skidding along the pavement at such a speed that the flagstones struck sparks from metal cleats on her boots. She was a strong woman and at length was able to wind Fido's chain around a lamppost that he had stopped to sniff. He went into a classical arabesque but, even in the midst of her difficulties, Mrs. Davies noted that this gesture was the merest formality. The dog was obviously saving his ammunition for a rainy day.

While she was at the climax of a sort of maypole routine around the lamppost, a policeman appeared. " 'Aving trouble, ma'am?" he asked. Mrs. Davies did not reply. It was obvious that he was amused at her discomfiture. "Bit of a handful, is 'e?"

Mrs. Davies stood still for a moment holding the chain with one hand and with the other trying to reach Fido's collar. She was afraid of officers of the law. She knew if ever she were seriously questioned by one that she would be totally at a loss as to how to reply. "I can manage, thank you," she said, slightly defensively.

" 'E's a fine fellow, ain't 'e?" The constable would have liked a little conversation or worse to wile away a minute or two in the monotony of the long night watch. He extended a fat hand to give the dog a public relations pat on the head. Fido bit him.

"Oh, you wicked boy," cried Mrs. Davies. "What ever are you doing?"

The policeman's face went scarlet. It hadn't far to go. Though only the thinnest trickle of blood was emerging from one knuckle, he held up his left hand like a one-armed Pekinese begging while with the other he explored his uniform for a handkerchief. This was located eventually in his left trouser pocket. He went through the motions of trying to reach it with his right hand, then, holding up the side of his tunic, he asked Mrs. Davies to assist. Now it was her turn to blush. Looking up and down the street to make sure that no one was looking, she cautiously lowered two fingers of the hand that was not holding the dog's chain, into the furnace of the policeman's trouser pocket. All the while, though her gaze was modestly averted, she was aware that the law was watching her from under his podgy eyelids.

"I'm sorry, officer," said Mrs. Davies dutifully rather than with sympathy.

"You should 'ave warned me, shouldn't you?"

"He's never done anything like that before. I can't think what came over him."

" 'E should wear a muzzle. It's against the law to walk a dog that's dangerous in public."

The accused continued alternately to apologize to the constable and to upbraid Fido, who remained obviously unrepentant.

"You're from the Great House, aren't you?"

Mrs. Davies bowed her head; no reply was needed.

"Yes. Well, if I've suffered any permanent damages, you'll be hearing from us."

At last, Mrs. Davies was free to grab Fido's collar and drag him home, but not without his tearing her skirt by snapping at it as they staggered along. She arrived back at the house with one of her black gloves split, her hat crooked, and her face bright orange with exertion and rage. As a way of preventing her life from becoming conspicuous, the outing had been a failure.

A Blessing
in Disguise

Raina's relationship with Fido was so unusual that she had supposed it to be outside the ordinary laws of cause and effect. She had therefore neglected to take certain standard contraceptive precautions. When Mr. Sylvester told Mr. Davies that she was unwell, she was, though no one knew it, suffering from morning sickness. As this mysterious condition did not abate, she went to see a doctor.

During the first visit, he asked her not to drench her body in perfume. It caused his eyes to water and made accurate examination difficult. As he said this he laughed but he did not sneer, for he liked her. In this he differed from most of the inhabitants of Ravenage, who, if they knew of her existence, hated Raina. She lived at a time when the enjoyment of sex was unfashionable. It was tolerated in men if they were discreet about it, but in women it was unthinkable. By these standards, Raina was a saint. She was almost entirely without vanity, without coquetry, and without lust. Like most of the house-wives in the city, she indulged man's appetites coldly, but unlike them, she never sank so low as to pander to their quite unjus-tified self-esteem.

The general animosity toward Raina was principally of two kinds. The younger women envied her. They thought of her as receiving the attentions of men without paying the price in monotony and domestic drudgery that was extorted from them every day of their lives. They never for a moment considered that she paid a different penalty. Until the arrival in her life of Mr. Sylvester, she had lived in constant danger. For inevitably prostitutes spend much of their time alone with men whose appearance or whose sexual habits are so repellent and so frightening that they dare not try to foist them upon women whom they know socially. Raina was truly a heroine.

Other townsfolk hated her brazenness rather than her sin. If she had behaved as though poverty had driven her to walking the streets, they could have pitied and even tried to redeem her. But her defiant attitude robbed them of this opportunity for self-indulgence. They argued that, if she so flagrantly demonstrated that she differed from other women, she must mean that she was better. They were wrong. Raina made almost no comparison between herself and other girls. She was self-regarding and, after considerable introspection, had long ago discovered herself to be lacking in maternal instinct and with very little capacity for tenderness. Accordingly she chose the profession for which the absence of these weaknesses qualified her. If the world had not reacted with such ludicrous disapproval, she would never have gone to such pains to shock it. She was like a child that only keeps on popping out from behind doors as long as its nanny continues to throw up her hands and squeak, "Oh, Miss Raina, you startled me."

Raina's life style challenged the fundamental mathematical tables by which society calculates its degrees of respectability. She was to ethics what Mr. Einstein would one day be to physics.

Perhaps it was because he usually saw women at their frailest that the doctor so admired Raina's strength and what could only be called her immoral courage. His liking for her was broad enough to enable him to feel free to comment on her bizarre appearance. She in turn was sufficiently detached to be able to enjoy his curiosity. At her second visit, when he confirmed her pregnancy, he said, "We've slipped up somewhere, haven't we?" His patient neither rejoiced nor wept; she let out a string of oaths so multifarious that even he failed to understand all of them. Her only question was, "How long will I be able to go on working?" "Until the labor pains start," her physician replied, "if you can find customers with concave stomachs." He touched the center of her belly with his pince-nez and added, "If it's a girl, she's going to have a very interesting life."

On her return home, she related the doctor's information to Mr. Sylvester. He too received the news more in anger than in sorrow. Even if clients of the shape described could be found, his wife would have to stop working for several weeks. Raina agreed that this would be so, but when he volunteered to make the traditional arrangement for disposing of their problem, to his amazement she refused to cooperate.

Husband and wife sat down opposite one another to discuss the matter calmly and reasonably but, within minutes, he was shouting at her and she was hitting him. She raised every moral, medical, and financial argument of which she could think. To all of them Mr. Sylvester found answers. Finally it transpired that her physical courage, although considerable, was not as great as her bravado. As near to tears as she was ever likely to be, she admitted that she was afraid. Long ago, at the age of fourteen, she had found herself in the same predicament as now. She was tried every remedy suggested (some of them maliciously) by all the people whose advice she had dared to ask. The resulting experience had been so horrible, the pain so excruciating, and the illness that followed so protracted that she was loath to take such a risk all over again. Finally, when the storm had passed, she agreed with her husband to think about the matter. As yet there was no need to make a decision.

A few days after this violent argument with his wife, Mr. Sylvester found the perfect solution to their problem. Taking all the money he could find, he left her.

For a while Raina continued to parade the streets. She felt both ill and depressed but, as neither a rosy complexion nor a sunny disposition had ever been among her attractions, the customers who only spent a short time with her noticed no difference. Mr. Davies was not among these. He paid higher fees than most of her clients and was therefore entitled to more of her time. He and especially Fido perceived the change in her at once. Her cynicism, once almost merry, was now morose— occasionally even savage. Obviously she wanted to entertain Davies less and less. At last, on one of his visits, she leaned over the sill of her front window and shouted into the street, "Not today," as though he were a gypsy selling flowers or an itinerant knife grinder.

After about a month of these half-hearted attempts to work, Raina could no longer bear the fatigue and the evening chill that are the inevitable consequences of an outdoor life. She took to staying at home, too depressed even to visit the doctor. Medically he could do little for her, but he cheered her up through his amoral attitude to life. She was slowly coming around to the idea that her husband had been right, but now he was nowhere to be found. Ultimately she was driven to confiding in her landlord. Because she had never shown any mercy, she therefore expected none. So she was very surprised when, without any fuss, he said she could stay in her rooms indefinitely and pay whatever she could. The snag to this arrangement was not the one she had anticipated. It was merely his continuous, fatherly presence in her front room when she was alone and in her back room on the now rare occasions when she had company.

He had inherited the house, but, even if he could have exchanged it for a bigger or a better one, he would not have done so. He could not have coped with the brisk, successful tenants that a house in a more fashionable street would have attracted. Failure was his natural setting. He did not want to crow over the misfortunes of others, nor to alleviate them. He surrounded himself with misfits because they confirmed his view that life was unfair.

Thus it came about that he was present when Raina went into labor. By her shaky reckoning she was only about a third of the way through her pregnancy, so she assumed that she was miscarrying. The situation seemed so grave that, for the first time anyone in Leman Street could remember, her landlord took off his carpet slippers and, wearing real shoes, went to fetch help. Remembering Raina's reaction when her worst fears had been confirmed, the doctor took it for granted that she had procured an abortion but he refrained from passing judgment and hurried to her bedside. Even so, by the time he arrived, Raina's union with Fido had been blessed. She had given birth to a child—well, perhaps it would be more accurate to call it a chuppy.

Raina's baby was male and so small that, when the doctor laid it on his hand, his fingertips supported its head and its legs lay along his wrist. He did not expect it to live more than a few minutes. In spite of this and although he knew it was un-wanted, he could not bring himself to treat it differently from any other newborn child. No preparation had been made for its arrival by its mother so, with a pocket handkerchief for a nappie, it was wrapped first in cotton wool, then swathed in various crepe-de-chine scarves and placed in a drawer taken out of its mother's dressing table. The landlord went out to buy a long list of things that would be required during the first few months of the infant's life. For three days, until he was sure that the child would live, to his own surprise and that of everyone who knew him, the old man remained sober in case an emergency should arise that demanded his unfuddled attention.

Raina endeavored to feed her baby from her shallow silvery breasts whose nipples looked like bites from ladylike

gnats, but it was meager fare and had to be augmented with milk from other sources.

Until now she had always thought that her slightest follies had been punished by fate with massive and totally disproportionate sentences. The birth of this child, which she had dreaded and the arguments for and against which she had pondered for so long, had been achieved so unexpectedly and with such ease that her melancholy mood passed overnight into one almost of joy.

As though it was an extension of her relief, a false spring blossomed over the entire countryside around Ravenage. The winter had been damp and dark rather than bitter. It required only sunlight for a whole season to pass away. For days the sky was pale blue from horizon to horizon. A white and windy sunshine redeemed the barren moorlands. Even the heights, where the grass was always dry and thin, were a grayish green. The farmers shook their heads silently, but in the town people became quite voluble. They even spoke to the Davieses. At the Great House, Mrs. Davies began to spring-clean for reasons other than to keep out of her husband's way. She would have liked to open all the windows in the house, but this she dared not do. Fido was in a restless mood and might have jumped out and disappeared.

Raina's arrangement with her landlord included the use of the garden at the back of the house. Until now this had meant nothing to her. She thought of the outdoors as only a vast marketplace where she could parade her wares. She never sat in it if this could be avoided. She was not a lover of nature.

Impressed by mere size, she had gone off real flowers as soon as she saw paper ones though this comparison was beside the point in Leman Street; the gardens there bloomed only with rubble and a few long-lost rubber balls. Their real purpose was as a space in which to park perambulators. There Raina left her child a great deal of the time, but she could not resist an occasional stroll along the pavement with her new perambulator. As she walked, she acted out the part of a fond mother, nodding, smiling, and chatting to her offspring, but she never for a moment took her consciousness away from the windows on the opposite side of the street. Though they watched with keen interest, none of the neighbors approached her, but a stranger to the district, an inveterate feeder of horses and patter of children's heads, made so bold as to peep under the fringed hood of the pram. "Is it a boy or a girl?" she asked. "Interested in his sex already?" the mother drawled. "He's a bit young."

Raina's high spirits were definitely returning. She felt better than she had for years and she knew that, in order to pay her debts, she must soon resume work, but she could not decide what to do about the child. She did not think she could rely on the landlord. His period of abstinence from alcohol was over. She missed her husband and was surprised that on her little excursions she never caught so much as a glimpse of him. She need not have worried. His spies were at work and, as soon as it was reported to him that his wife could once again walk, Mr. Sylvester returned.

Nowhere in Ravenage or in nearby towns had he been able

to discover girls half so dedicated as his wife. In the end they all became lazy, got drunk, fell in love, or in some other way disgraced themselves.

Raina could not be said to have taken him back. That would imply some gesture of forgiveness from her or, on his part, an act of contrition. He was reabsorbed into her life with as little disturbance as if he had been out for an extended walk. Only the landlord noticed the difference. Disgruntled, he re-occupied his own premises. For a moment he thought of forbidding Raina the use of the garden but he found that he hadn't the heart.

Except as a means of arousing the shocked curiosity of the neighbors, the Sylvesters were going to find out that there was very little to be said for parenthood. But, for a while after their unemphatic reunion, they regarded as comic the stereotyped domestic tableau in which they found themselves. The child seemed little more than a toy given to them by a practical joker. They addressed each other as "Mummy" and "Daddy" and Raina fell about the room laughing. Even the infant's unprepossessing appearance was the subject of jokes in which the parents attributed their offspring's worst feature to each other. They were voluble with mutual assurance that all newborn babies looked like lobsters. Then one of the few neighbors who was on their side looked into the perambulator and said, "Doesn't he look—um—ar—comfortable." Gradually the parents stopped laughing; the quips became fewer until at last by tacit agreement all references to the child's face became taboo.

Facing the
Consequences

The only visitor to the house whose attitude toward the baby was unequivocally sanguine was Fido. On one occasion, while Davies watched with wonder and Raina with anxiety, the dog took hold of the child's clothes with his teeth and, lifting it out of the cot, brought it to its mother.

With the change in the weather and the uplifting of Raina's spirits, she had graciously consented to Davies' resumption of his visits. She allowed him to lie on the bed beside her and listen as before to the wicked tales that she loved to tell. Provided that Mr. Sylvester never heard about it, she agreed to charge him only the amount he had paid on his first visits. This was the nearest she was ever going to come to a gesture of friendship.

But she wanted nothing more to do with Fido. There were several reasons for this. She was by nature fickle and, now that her husband had returned, she needed all her energy for meeting the demands he made upon her. He seemed determined that she should make up for lost revenue. He introduced her to clients in such rapid succession that what she had chosen as an exotic and very personal profession was rapidly becoming conveyor-belt work. She was turning into a chain prostitute, lighting each new customer from the stub of the last. The most repellent aspect of the dog's advances, however, was the fact that his master had come to the end of his savings. Raina was not nearly as mercenary as her husband. She never uttered words such as "overhead" or "depreciation," which were forever on his lips, but she was what in modern parlance would be called "coin-op." She hated to be compelled to lift a finger—let alone any other part of the body—without being paid at least something. If she did anything for nothing, it might seem that she liked someone. This would never do. She was a puritan at heart.

Mr. Davies did not know what to do with friendship. He accepted the new relationship sadly, even with embarrassment, while hoping for a miracle. The dog's reactions were more emphatic. He became bewildered at first, then importunate, and finally angry. He made impermissible overtures to Raina and, when she pushed him out of the way, he snapped at her. She had not greatly resented the affront to her womanhood but was furious to see a ladder running down her stocking. She told Davies that in the future he must visit her alone. He thanked her politely, but the sidelong glance and the simpering expression had left his face.

If Davies had never experienced anything more exciting, occasional conversations with a prostitute might have seemed wonderful; but now they seemed an anticlimax, and gradually he ceased to go to Leman Street.

Fido became a prisoner; his exercise yard was the back garden of the Great House. There he flung himself against the side gate, tried to burrow under the wire fence, and generally became such a nuisance that Davies decided that he must at least try to alleviate the dog's restlessness.

Because his dreams and real life had recently drawn closer together, even overlapped, this archetypical slave had developed something almost like strength of character. He could not as yet summon up sufficient effrontery to ask Mr. Minguillan to disburse funds for the enrichment of Fido's peculiar nightlife, but during the lawyer's next visit he did suggest that the dog be mated in a more conventional way. Mr. Minguillan found this notion ludicrous. "What would be the point?" he asked, perfidiously patting Fido's head. "Appealing as our friend may be, for one thing he is not full grown and, for another, he is no thoroughbred. The puppies would be valueless—worse, a nuisance—worse still, an expense." He had various lucrative ways of investing Lord Emms' money and did not wish these to be diminished by so much as a penny.

For the first time in his life, Davies answered back to someone richer than himself. He said that he had distinctly heard his late master say that Fido must have puppies.

Mr. Minguillan winked at the dog and replied, "I've no objection to him working out something for himself at an amateur level, but anything else would be a flagrant misinterpretation of your late, lamented employer's will. I'm sure you wouldn't want anything of that kind."

Davies would have liked nothing better, but he remained silent. His future seemed likely to become so boring that he thought seriously of taking the lawyer's advice and planting a few seeds in the kitchen garden.

The only person whose lot seemed to have improved was

CHOG

his wife. She had never been able to bring herself to mention
Leman Street, but as though by a miracle, Davies had begun to
go out less, and never at night with the dog. The scandal which
she had seen gathering on the horizon like a hurricane and
which she thought must inevitably engulf her was blowing
over. She no longer felt the need to stare at the pavement when
she went out.

She had lately given up shopping in the morning. It had
upset her routine, but it made her less likely to encounter Mrs.
Adie, with whom her last meeting had been so painful, first,
because it was then that she had learned of her husband's
disgraceful behavior and, second, because she had reacted to
the news with such lack of self-control. Even in the afternoon
she was obliged more than once to hurry past a shop in which
she saw her friend being served or to stare at goods she had no
intention of buying until the danger had passed by on the other
side of the road.

Now she began once more to walk into the town soon after
breakfast. It was not long before she came face to face with her
friend. "We haven't bumped into each other for ages," said
Mrs. Adie, who knew perfectly well that she had been avoided.
Mrs. Davies smiled. Although for days she had been hoping for
this meeting, she had prepared no explanation for her change
of routine. "You must come and see me for one of our little
suppers," said her friend. Mrs. Davies thanked her. After a few
more of these chance encounters, the two women agreed on an
actual date.

Mrs. Davies dearly longed to take with her a present to lighten the moral burden she felt when she thought of all those unreturned visits, but she could not think what. In the days when there were flowers in the garden and fruit on the trees this problem would have been easier to solve. After lengthy cogitation she decided to make some fudge according to the recipe the cook had shown her back when Lord Emms' son was alive. Though Mrs. Adie could not resist saying that sweets would make her fat, the gift was well enough received for the guilt to slip from Mrs. Davies' shoulders.

When the twitters of gratitude and the murmurs of self-deprecation were over, the two ladies sat down to an elaborate high tea. Mrs. Adie changed her room slightly at the beginning of every April. The table with the snowy cloth was moved farther from the fire and nearer to the window, which this evening was open. This turned out to be a mistake. When the lamp was lit, the feast was invaded by a hideous insect.

"How is Mr. Davies?" the hostess asked as if the idea of him had just popped into her head.

"He's better, thank you," Mrs. Davies replied.

"Oh, he's been ill then," said the hostess, with the minimum of concern permissible for the occasion.

"He doesn't seem so restless." Mrs. Davies was pulling with all her might on the rudder of this conversation to steer it toward the desired shore without its foundering on the jagged rocks of actual statement. Mrs. Adie decided to help. "And that strange dog of his?"

"We keep him in the garden now that the weather is so much better." This was as near as she dared go to saying that a scandal had been averted.

"How nice!" This comment did not mean that Mrs. Adie had forgiven Davies. On the doorstep, when it was suggested that she should visit the Great House the following week, she gave her departing guest a fleeting glance and said, "We'll see."

As she walked slowly through the warm, blowy evening, Mrs. Davies reflected on these words. She had been comforted by the encounter but also baffled. She and her best friend were both women, both housekeepers and, though she was well aware that Mrs. Adie looked much younger, they were much the same age but, in some unfathomable way, they were not equal. They never would be.

While the Sylvesters' interest in family life grew fainter and fainter, their child waxed steadily stronger. In spite of a diet that it would have been kind to call experimental, it put on weight at a pace which, if the doctor had been watching, he would have described as phenomenal. When only three months old, the infant could jump on its mother's lap to be fed; at twice that age it had sufficient strength to fling the landlord's cat against the garden wall so hard that it died on the spot.

The chuppy was fast becoming a chog.

Being quite unused to the rearing of children, its parents had no idea how lucky they were. Their baby never cried. In whatever discomfort and however long neglected, it only grizzled, making a soft, high sound inside its nose, which they soon learned to ignore. Moreover, it was surprisingly self-sufficient, demanding no bright, ingenious toys but content to play with a dry stick from the garden or one of its mother's old shoes. Whatever it was given and some things that it was not, it tore to pieces in the end. Already it was displaying quite a flair for destruction.

The death of the cat momentarily aroused the landlord to protest. His prurient curiosity about his upstairs lodgers, the odd sounds that came through the ceiling, the amusing glimpses of their departing clients, did not compensate him for the loss of his only friend. Mr. Sylvester dismissed his grievance by thrusting a half crown into his hand and saying, "Cheer up, granddad. Buy yourself another."

The injured party took the money, which he later spent on drink, but he still felt that his delicate feelings had been trampled underfoot. "You think you can do anything you like here," he said, "but you can't. You're on sufferance, d'you know that?"

"We pay our rent."

Raina heard her husband say this. Sure that appeasement was needed rather than defiance, she came out of her room onto the landing. "It was an accident," she explained. She leaned against the doorpost with her peignoir undone down to her knees. She usually found that this added strength to any argument that she cared to advance. "The kid didn't mean any harm."

For once her ruse had no effect. "If I went to the police, you two would be in real trouble," the landlord said.

Though the target was small, this shaft pierced Mr. Sylvester to the heart. He was more afraid of the law than was his wife, and not without cause. Raina's experience of policemen was that most charges were dropped if she took the arresting officer into a dark doorway. But her husband was less fortunate. For one thing, it would be a very rare constable whom he could appease with this simple device and, for another, the offense of living off the immoral earnings of a woman was considered far more serious than mere prostitution.

The landlord's words, which in fact the fuddled old man would later forget, had the effect on the Sylvesters of bringing to the forefront of their thoughts a scheme which until now they had often discussed but only as a wistful possibility. They wanted to move on to a bigger town—preferably London. Raina was of two minds about the prospect. She longed for the glamour which she was sure spangled the night life of all capital cities, but she knew that in a vast populace she could not hope to be the nucleus of so much gossip as she was in Ravenage. She would miss that. Her husband had no such reservations. He felt certain that, given half a chance, he could acquire a whole stable of girls without nearly as much risk of detection as he ran in a county town. Moreover, dotted across a huge area like London, his employees need never know about one another. This would avoid those jealous scenes in which in his youth he had so often been involved and which he found not flattering but tiring. For the Sylvesters, Ravenage was finished. What with her exhibitionism and his avarice they had plowed the thin soil of this small cathedral city so thriftlessly that it had become a dust bowl of sin.

Having a change of venue in mind and with the extra expense that the move would incur pressing upon them, their child became nothing more than excess baggage. Looked at through the wrong end of a telescope he was a prodigy, but his parents could not blind themselves to the fact that he already took up a great deal of their time and would soon take up an even greater portion of their income. A situation which had appeared irksome for some time now seemed desperate. It demanded a desperate remedy.

Among the few neighbors who were not ashamed to speak to them, the Sylvesters spread the news that, in spite of conspicuous evidence to the contrary, their child was ailing and must go to its grandparents in an unspecified part of the country to recuperate. By the time there was any speculation as to why the boy had never returned, its parents would have slipped away to London.

There were in the very nature of things certain days on which Raina did not work. Usually, at these times, if she was not well enough to accompany her husband to the music hall or a race course, they sat at home playing cards or having a row or both. On the next such day of enforced idleness, she decided that, instead of indulging in any of these pleasant pastimes, she would deal with the family problem. She warned her husband well in advance, assuming that he would assist her in the difficult work that had to be done. At the last minute he staged a Macbeth and retired into the back room.

If ever Raina had come near to making friends, it had always been with men weaker than herself; she preferred the effortlessness of their company. This predilection had its disadvantages. In every crisis that she could remember, she had always been alone. She was alone now.

Fido Strikes

Though she never fully formulated the thought, Mrs. Davies had for many years assumed that her husband had become sexless. Having had no experience of any man but him and never having spoken explicitly about sex to anyone, she had supposed this to be part of the aging process. She was glad that it was so. It saved a lot of bother. At one time she had even hoped that it might help them to become friends. Now that the Leman Street scandal had been mentioned, she was forced to rearrange all her ideas about him. He was sexless only with her.

To Mrs. Davies a respectable life was not only desirable; it was natural. She had no pity for sexual or any other kind of excess because she felt no temptation. When she read in the papers about murder or rape or robbery, she was suitably shocked. She was also amazed. Instead of seeing the perpetrators of these crimes as having given way to impulses that they could no longer control, she marveled at the ingenuity and the energy that these strange creatures had been able to summon up for the performance of these far-fetched acts. Now, though her husband had committed no crime, she must number him among these bizarre people.

To win back Mrs. Adie's friendship or at least her acceptance, Mrs. Davies had managed to communicate, though hardly to state, that her husband had ceased to go to Leman Street. She certainly hoped that this was true, but she knew that she was never again going to be able to take anything he did or said for granted. From now on she must keep watch, but her vigilance was fitful. Some days she forgot all about her husband's secret desires and even about the dog's mounting hostility. If the afternoons were fine, she strolled along the overgrown paths of the garden and watched Fido gamboling on the lawn. She would even throw a stick for him to fetch. Only when he stood still and stared at her scornfully did she remember that the happier phase of their relationship was ended. The innocent games were past. She would even help her husband weed the kitchen garden or sit on the garden roller while she asked him what he would like for supper. But then some simple observation would call forth from him a caustic reply, and her doubts about him would return.

She connected his excursions into a life of sin with nighttime, and therefore never tried to prevent his going out during daylight hours. Also, because Mrs. Adie had laid such stress upon the conspicuousness of Fido, Mrs. Davies associated the dog with the visits to Leman Street. If her husband went out alone, it did not disturb her. She never questioned these preconceptions but sometimes, when she was alone, even she became aware to what extent she was a victim of her moods. The thought worried her. She tried to find in herself some hard core of identity which was not subject to changes in the weather or her husband's irascibility, but in vain. Inevitably vigilance at the mercy of so many whims must fail before long.

One summer evening after supper, she fell asleep in the

basket chair in the kitchen. Perhaps because she had eaten some cream cheese that she herself had made, she was plunged into a hideous nightmare involving the policeman whom she had met when she tried to take Fido for a walk. In her dream she opened the front door to find the officer on the steps. Behind him stood a crowd of townsfolk as brightly illuminated as if all the lights in the house were on. Among them were Davies and the dog staring at her as though she were to blame for she knew not what. There was a clanking sound as the constable produced a huge pair of handcuffs. She woke.

Her husband was not sitting opposite her as he had been minutes, or possibly hours, ago. Her suspicions instantly aroused, she staggered into the hall to see him stooping by the open door to affix Fido's chain to his collar.

"Where are you going? What are you doing?" she asked, unable to keep the panic from her voice. As these questions shot from her lips, she took up a defiant posture in the doorway with her arms outstretched.

Davies stood before her with his mouth open, one hand holding the dog's chain and the other in the sleeve of his mackintosh. It was a warm night, but he had made it a rule never to go into the street without at least carrying a coat of some kind. Whatever his mission, to be seen outdoors in purely indoor clothing would have been in his judgment a breach of decorum. "What's got into you?" he gasped. He stared at his wife in amazement—even in terror. For some time, he had been coming to the conclusion that she was losing her reason. Now that fear became a certainty.

"No," she kept saying. "No. Don't go."

"It's a nice evening. I haven't taken him out for ages. What's the matter with you?"

"You're going to Leman Street." Mrs. Davies had not thought that she would ever be able to pronounce the words so loaded with degradation. Now that she had, she felt relieved—almost exhilarated.

"Leman Street," her husband repeated almost in a whisper.

"You're a fool, a laughing stock."

"How do you know about Leman Street?"

"Everyone knows. That house."

It seemed that there was no longer any use feigning innocence. Davies tried conciliation. "That house. For heaven's sake. Nothing happened."

Mrs. Davies could well believe it. Nothing had happened in her marriage for years. This did not in her eyes diminish her husband's iniquity. "The disgrace," she hissed. "The scandal." She was glad to see that her adversary was nonplussed.

Her triumph was short-lived. Mr. Davies had stepped back to the wall opposite the front door. Like a fierce jet of water, the barrage of accusations seemed to have forced him to retreat. It could never be said afterward that he deliberately set the dog on her, but he certainly let go of the chain at which Fido was now straining. The dog had become aware that Mrs. Davies

was endeavoring to bar his way to the front garden and to freedom. He leaped forward. Mrs. Davies managed to ward off his bared teeth by thrusting both hands instinctively toward him, but one of his huge paws slipped through this defense, struck her eye, and slid down her cheek. As she fell back onto the steps clutching her face, the dog bounded over her and raced toward the gates.

Davies made a feeble effort to call the dog back, began to run after him, then turned and bent down to look at his wife. She was still alive. Taking her by the shoulders, he attempted to lift her up, more angry at her dead weight than sorry for her plight. She moaned faintly with her mouth open and her head lolling about on her shoulders like that of a rag doll. The blood oozing from her eye disgusted him. He felt sick and totally inadequate to deal with the situation in which she had so unfairly involved him. After dragging her body and propping it against the doorpost like a Guy Fawkes effigy, he straightened his back and struggled into his mackintosh. He could not concentrate on any course of action. His real anxiety was not about his wife but about Fido. What would become of him if the dog were to disappear altogether or be run over? After standing for a moment in a state of dithering indecision, he trundled down the drive.

Mrs. Davies had not screamed as her head struck the stone steps, because the impact had knocked her unconscious. When she regained her senses, she felt cold and one side of her face was wet, but as yet she felt no pain. With difficulty she scrambled to her feet and lurched into the house. There was a tiny washroom just inside by the front door. Here she dipped the corner of her apron into a basin of water and dabbed cautiously at her cheek. Then she lifted up her face to the window, through which the violet sky glowed dimly. Very slowly she put one hand over her undamaged eye. The room went black. "It's blind," she whispered.

Her confrontation with her husband had been delayed too long. Mrs. Adie had wasted too much time choosing sufficiently delicate words to impart indelicate news, because she genuinely wished to warn her friend but only if it could be done without the least display of vulgar curiosity. Mrs. Davies herself had hesitated unduly before accusing her husband of his sin. By the time she had made her haphazard protest, he was an addict of his peculiar perversity and the dog had become confirmed in its ambition. Fido's association with a woman had given him a sense of triumph. It had changed him from a tease into a tyrant. Corruption bestows power; total corruption gives unlimited power.

Raina had waited for evening partly out of reluctance to begin the unpleasant task that lay before her and partly in the hope that by then her landlord would be immersed in a golden cloud of alcohol. He was, but even so, he noticed that Fido had arrived at the house without his master. This had never happened before. The event made him sufficiently curious to shuffle to the door and look up and down the street to see if Mr. Davies was anywhere to be seen.

The dog edged past him and darted up the stairs. He was already on the landing when Raina, hearing the front door click, decided to reconnoiter. Although she opened the door of her room only a few inches, the invader forced his head into the aperture. Recently Raina had treated the dog contemptuously, but she had never hurt him. Now, in a highly nervous state, she kicked his nose with her gilded shoe. In retaliation he snapped at her ankle. She cursed but, still hoping not to cause a commotion, did not cry out. She backed onto the great bed, where for a moment she tottered unsteadily, realizing that the situation was altogether more serious than she had at first thought. She was used to seeing this animal looking petulant; suddenly he was savage. His entire face was furrowed by the force with which the flesh was drawn back over his glistening teeth. He did not bark but, which was far more frightening, growled continually. Jumping off the far side of the bed, Raina picked up the frail chair from in front of her dressing table. As the dog sprung clear across the bed, she swung back the chair to strike him. It shattered the window and two of its spiky legs caught in the lace curtain. She never dealt the intended blow. Her brittle skeletal frame was crushed to the floor by the massive weight of the dog. With her mouth agape, she turned her head away toward the broken window but she did not scream. Fido was gnawing through her windpipe.

Mr. Sylvester recognized the sound of splintering glass as being more than one would expect from a routine sexual encounter. As he had once promised his wife that he would be, he was through the wardrobe and into the front room in a flash, the razor waving before him. Fido didn't have a dog's chance. Before he could turn his attention from shaking Raina like a dead rat, he had received the first swift cut on the side of his neck. Dazed for a moment by the pain, he turned too slowly before trying to bite the crimson blade. In an instant his muzzle was slashed from ear to ear. Mr. Sylvester was indeed, as he had boasted, an expert with his chosen weapon. Even so, it took all his skill to defeat an enemy whose movements seemed to be inspired less by a desire to survive than by a reckless demoniac rage. In the narrow space between the window and the bed, Raina's sticklike limbs twitched as man and dog trampled over her body. Her eyes stared out of pools of mascara and on her parted lips the scarlet make-up and the blood were undistinguishable. In the darkness there was no barking and no shouting. After a few minutes there was not even the thud of stumbling limbs or the sound of breaking furniture. Fido was dead.

All this time the lodgers on the top floor had stood with their ears pressed to their locked doors. Not until silence was fully restored did they venture out onto the landing. They looked down, though not in mercy.

Only the landlord, after falling back down the stairs twice, had nerve enough to make his way to the field of battle. As he entered Raina's front room, everything near the door looked surprisingly calm. All he could see beyond the bed was the motionless figure of Raina's husband silhouetted against the livid light of the lamps in Leman Street.

"What the hell?" said the landlord very quietly. Then he crossed the darkened room and looked down. Mr. Sylvester said nothing. All he wanted to do was to escape, but he remained standing with the razor still open in his hand. Where could he go? How could he hide? He was drenched in blood. It was even on his gray suede shoes. Hopelessly he turned toward the broken window, through which the evening breeze blew cool on his wet face. A crowd was already gathering in the street below like corpuscles around a septic wound. When they looked up, through the shreds of curtain they saw a man's pale eyes stare down at them from a vermilion mask. They screamed.

To the people who lived opposite her, Raina's life had been like a serial story in a women's magazine. Each installment had been more exciting than the last. She had arrived; she had begun her wicked life; she had married; she had produced a baby; and now, though it would be hours before there was any proof, they were sure she had met a violent death. They were genuinely afraid at seeing the hand of fate at work, but they were also delighted. Every catastrophe is a passover feast for those not involved. Their sins remain hidden from the furies for yet one more day; their mad risks have been smiled upon so far by fortune. As a rule this hideous joy must be expressed obliquely. Receivers of bad news must murmur, "How terrible!" or "Poor thing." Apparently God is thought to be more easily deceived than we are, who know that what is meant is the opposite of what is said. Raina's death was special—just as she would have wished it to be. It demanded no hypocritical mumblings. At last to Leman Street had come a disaster in which everyone could rejoice openly; nobody could be blamed for being heartless.

So as to be able to digest every last morsel of the event, people remained in the street so long that the women became tired and sat on the steps of houses to whose owners as a rule they barely nodded. When the landlord lit the gas in the second-floor front room, the eyes of the spectators burst into a hundred tiny flames, when a shadow on the ceiling indicated a movement within the room, pointing fingers shot up from the crowd like bristles on the back of a frightened animal, voices twittered, hands clutched at the nearest sleeve. The entire mass of people gasped, shuddered, swayed in an ecstasy of cruel neighborliness.

In this feverish atmosphere it was not unusual that the arrival of Mr. Davies at the far end of the street passed unnoticed. He turned the corner breathless, having trotted from home when he thought no one was looking and walked as fast as he could when he felt he was attracting attention. Stealthily he approached Raina's house, along the opposite side of the road. Even at a discreet distance he could clearly see that the window had been smashed and the lace curtain torn to shreds. In all the commotion there was neither sight nor sound of Fido but an instinct warned him that the dog was somehow involved. Mr. Davies was sick with fear and yet consumed with hideous curiosity. As he stood staring at the house, his heart became a

battlefield for two ambitions that had largely ruled his life—
the desire never to be mixed up in anything that was not
respectable and the wish never to lose sight of a steady, more or
less effortless income. He braced himself to cross the road and
mingle with the outer fringe of the crowd, which, consisting of
latecomers who did not live close-by were less likely to recog-
nize him.

As he stepped off the curb he noticed a policeman approaching from the other end of the street at a ludicrously
dignified pace. As inconspicuously as possible, Mr. Davies
turned back. He tried to convince himself that Fido would be at
home when he returned to the Great House, but he was filled
with foreboding. With leaden steps he turned into the main
road, relieved only to be out of sight of the crowd. He had gone
but a few yards when, immediately in front of him, appeared
Chog.

Chog Makes
Himself
at Home

All day long this strange creature had been aware of the danger that charged the scented air of his mother's room. She had tried to feed him with substances that his nose warned him to avoid; she had insisted that he lie down when as a rule she was indifferent to the lateness of the hour; and, however much he tried to provoke either of his parents, they did not shout at him or chase him around the room. Worst of all, at no time since dawn had he been allowed in the garden.

When all of a sudden the growling and the cursing began, he had been lying very still with his eyes open and his gaze wandering about the room. At once, he crawled under the bed. As soon as the fighting started in earnest, he scuttled through the open door, down the stairs, and into the hall. At ground level he made straight for the garden. Here he had never encountered anyone except his mother. He regarded the place as his very own territory. To look over the back wall, he had often climbed the heap of sand and broken bricks that were piled up in one corner. Today, for the first time, driven by panic, he jumped down the other side. He landed on the asphalt path on his feet and hands. Although his palms were unnaturally hard, they stung for a moment as they struck the ground. Otherwise he was unhurt. But he was more afraid than before. In almost total darkness, he began to run this way and that, poking his head through apertures in broken fences but not venturing to scramble into unknown back gardens.

Twice he returned to the brick wall of his own kingdom but, from the outside, it was too high for him to climb. He began to make the high-pitched noise inside his nose that expressed his grief. Then he saw the street lamps shining at the end of the alleyway. He ran toward them.

In the main road, he was stricken by a different kind of panic. Here the light was as frightening as before the darkness had been and the people were too numerous. A sudden prey to indecision, he looked up and down the street with his head held high and his nose faintly wrinkled. Mr. Davies was standing stock-still in the hope of thus avoiding attention. The ruse did not work. Chog saw him instantly. He ran forward, jumped up, and clung about his waist like a vast watch chain. The frail little man nearly fell backward. "Down," he commanded harshly. "Down." He began to strike the child's arms with his fist until he saw a passer-by smiling benignly at what she thought was a game. He composed himself somewhat and put the child down with studied forbearance. Then he walked on dreadfully unconcerned.

His unwanted companion was not to be put off. He had learned to depend on grown-up people but not to trust them. Though Davies neither looked in his direction nor spoke a single word to him, he ran before, behind, and around him, constantly watching his face. When they reached the dignified quietude of the road leading to the Great House, Davies picked up a stone and threw it at his pursuer. His aim was so poor that Chog had to run several yards to fetch the missile and bring it to his playmate. This gave Davies an idea. When they arrived at the front door, turning what had originally been meant to be a battle into a gesture of friendship, he found a pebble and, smiling, lobbed it into the distance. While it was being retrieved, there was time to slip into the house.

As he looked back in triumph, he noticed the blood on the steps. The misery of the situation from which he had fled only half an hour earlier poured over him like filthy water. In the hall he paused for a long time before walking slowly into the kitchen. There, as he had guessed, he found his wife sitting at the table with cotton wool, boric acid, and a small basin of water before her. As he entered the room, though the water was now cold, she began to bathe her eye again. "I'm blind," she said.

"He's gone," Davies replied. He was revolted by any kind of disfigurement and made no pretense of examining his wife's wound, but he was compelled to bandage her head. She could not do it for herself. She had to insert a finger between her temple and the bandage to prevent him from tying it so tight that it hurt. While he went upstairs to find a safety pin, Mrs. Davies, hearing a sound outside the front door, went to investigate. Her husband heard her, leaned over the banister, and shouted, "No."

"It's Fido," she called back.

"No!" commanded Mr. Davies ever more sternly but with no more effect.

His wife opened the door.

There stood Chog.

Even with one eye, Mrs. Davies could see that something was amiss. Her momentary hesitation was sufficient to allow the child to squeeze into the house. Davies was downstairs in a matter of seconds. "It can't stay here," he said. The idea of the two separate compartments of his life being thrown open to each other by this go-between was intolerable. Unable to bring himself to touch the creature, he went and stood by the open door. "Out," he said, pointing into the darkness. "Out." The child took no notice but continued to run about the great hall, looking at everything, touching everything. Davies took one of Lord Emms' walking sticks from the umbrella stand and brandished it feebly.

Now it was Mrs. Davies' turn to cry, "No. No." She put her hand on the child's head and guided it gently into the kitchen. "You can't turn him out at this time of night," she protested. She sat down in the wicker chair and forced herself to take the child onto her lap. Immediately he flung himself on her bosom and kissed her chin. Davies sat at the table and surveyed this scene with disgust but could not quite bring himself to struggle with his wife for possession of the child. The loss of dignity would be too great. Besides, he might not win.

Mrs. Davies was grimly aware that her husband did not like children. Even so, his reactions seemed exaggerated. "What's the matter?" she asked. "What is it?"

"It's nothing. I don't know what you're talking about."

"If you want to get rid of the poor little mite, why don't you go around to the police station and tell them . . ."

"No," said Davies yet again. "We can't do that."

He spoke too fast and too emphatically. His desperate manner aroused his wife's suspicions. "Why ever not? We haven't done anything. We're not in the wrong. They'd thank us," she added with a trace of smugness. Mrs. Davies imagined that the right way to deal with authority was to ingratiate herself with it; Davies, more worldly than his wife, thought it wiser merely to keep out of its way.

"They'd ask questions. They'd want to know why the wretched creature's here, miles from—from anywhere." It was foolish to have added these words.

"Miles from where? Miles from his home? Where does he come from?"

"I don't know. How could I?"

"You do know."

The accusations and denials flew back and forth across the table while the child dozed fitfully in her lap. Gradually the truth dawned on Mrs. Davies. Her husband had gone to Leman Street in spite of all her protests, and it was from there that the child had followed him. How could it have been otherwise? "He's hers," she said, in a grating whisper. "He's that woman's child." Abruptly she allowed Chog to slide from her knees onto the hearth rug. He made several bold attempts to jump back. To prevent him from succeeding, Mrs. Davies jerked her chair around until her legs were partially under the table. She pressed the palm of one hand over her bandaged eye and sobbed loudly and without restraint. Her husband, hating her for embarrassing him, said nothing.

After a while, Mrs. Davies rose to her feet. She was a little calmer but the tears still flowed. She put a small saucepan on the range with some milk in it. Then from the larder she fetched a loaf of bread, cut a slice from it, chopped this into cubes, put them in a little bowl, and covered them with brown sugar. All the while, she was scrutinizing the child. The longer she looked, the more mystified she became. Surely, she thought, he could not be her husband's. He was so big that he seemed to be about four years old—and yet he never spoke. His appearance was so strange that it was difficult to make any judgments. "A person like that," she said, "having children. It's wicked."

"She's a married woman," Mr. Davies remarked, and to lessen the talltale certainty of his remark, added lamely, "apparently."

"A husband. What kind of man would marry a woman like that?"

"Don't ask me. I hardly ever saw him." Though each of his replies was a denial of any but the most superficial knowledge of Raina's circumstances, every word he uttered drew from him some unintended admission of gross familiarity. His wife could not bring herself to look at him. She was ashamed not only of his sin but of the feebleness of his attempts to cover it up. Unaccountably her mind darted back to memories of her early married life. How empty it had been! How soon she had ceased to expect any affirmation of their professed oneness! Her mind flinched from any contemplation of their sexual relationship not only out of prudishness but out of despair as well. No wonder she had never had children. But this woman in Leman Street had. "God will punish her," she said, the vehemence of her tone being made to compensate for the lack of any real hope that her wish would be fulfilled.

In spite of the turmoil in her heart, she sat patiently and fed the child the bread and milk. Life continues not because of any sustained optimism but by means of habits formed when some hope at least is present. The child bolted its food with an energy that shocked her. "The poor thing's starving," she said. "I don't suppose she ever fed it properly."

Mrs. Davies felt pity at seeing the intensity of the child's hunger but, when his supper was finished, her sense of refinement prevented her from allowing him to lick the bowl from which she had fed him. It was important to her that she seem very different from his mother. She led him upstairs to one of the rooms that she so conscientiously kept aired and sat him on the edge of the bed. She was extremely tired but she was determined to do right by the poor waif whom chance had placed in her care. His body was lean and angular and his skin was covered with a fine, almost invisible down. She showed no sign that this surprised her. It was not until she removed his shoes and saw the shape of his feet that she fainted.

Even now, in spite of the change or, rather, the reversal of their feelings about one another, the Davieses still slept in the same bed. There were any number of rooms into which either of them could have moved but, since they never discussed their relationship, they could never come to an arrangement that calmly expressed the antipathy each knew the other felt. If either of them had suddenly left the marriage bed while the other stayed, the one making the gesture of rebellion would have become the accuser; the other would by default have been the guilty party. The decision would have been interpreted by one or the other as referring to some single act of disloyalty or some insulting word that had just been done or said. Neither husband nor wife wished it to seem that anything the other could do could increase the intensity of their mutual hostility, The propinquity that had once been a symbol of their solidarity was now a sign of their contempt.

Far into the night, though Mrs. Davies was worn out with pain and misery, discussion continued concerning Fido. In the dark, no longer facing one another, the condemnatory tone of their discourse abated. They did not converse so much as abandon themselves to loosely interlocking soliloquies. Once Davies had been led into an admission that he had gone straight to Leman Street because he knew it was the place where Fido would almost certainly be found, he could without further self-incrimination describe what he had seen there. Even his wife realized that he could not safely tarry at the scene of the disaster. If the dog had gone there and did not return of its own accord, it would almost certainly be brought back to the Great House by someone.

"Why?" Mrs. Davies asked, by now too sleepy to think even as logically as she usually did.

"Because of his collar," her husband explained.

Mrs. Davies uttered a faint moan. On the inside of her aching eyelid appeared the words that when she had first read them had so amazed her: "FIDO—I trust no one but Lord Emms." She tried to imagine whether the shame of having the dog returned from a place of ill repute by a stranger would be outweighed by the relief at seeing their only source of income restored.

The chief cause of weary contention between the Davieses was that Mrs. Davies thought that her husband should go to the police in the morning, while he was in favor of waiting a short but undefined period in the hope of a miracle. They were spared having to reach a decision on this point. A police inspector came to see them.

Even if Fido had not been wearing his famous collar, the police would have had no difficulty in tracing its owner. There had been no shortage of people at the scene of the crime willing, even eager, to describe in detail what men at what hour of night had stayed how long in Raina's company, and of all these subjects of local speculation none was more conspicuous than the man with the dog. He was described variously as comical, sinister, and ordinary, and the animal with him as sweet and fierce. Everyone knew something about him or thought they did, and some knew that he and his wife still lived in what were called mysterious circumstances in the house where once they had merely been servants.

That it was Raina's body that was being removed from the house in Leman Street was something that bystanders could

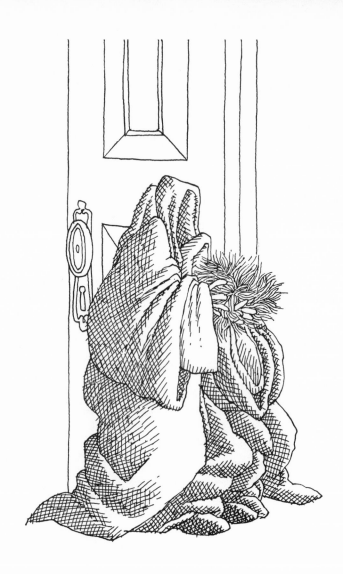

only guess, but it was not a difficult presumption to make. The sheet lay almost flat over the stretcher. Either the lightness of her limbs or of her morals seemed to free the police from dealing with her corpse with any particular solemnity. Partly because of this, the onlookers uttered only a perfunctory murmur as she was shoveled into the ambulance. It was not until Fido's lacerated body was brought out into the street that like a disturbed swarm of bees, a funereal groan rose above the crowd.

The inspector dealing with the case was fully aware of the peculiarity in the English character exemplified by this reaction. On his way to the Davieses to inform them of their bereavement, like an actor in the wings, he lowered himself carefully into his tragic register.

Normally the crunch of horses' hooves on the gravel outside the Great House heralded nothing more portentous than the delivery of Fido's steak. Today this noise filled Davies with almost uncontrollable agitation. All morning, from one front window or another, he had been maintaining an intermittent vigil. Immediately on hearing these sounds from the outer world, he ordered Mrs. Davies to take the child into a bedroom and keep it there. His policy was the opposite of his wife's. He did not hope to rid himself of all his problems with a single abandoned gesture. He preferred to cope with each of them separately and with great caution. Moving out of sight, he watched a stranger alight from a black vehicle and, followed by an attendant, march with great deliberation to the front steps.

Mr. Davies then hurried downstairs to face a crisis of whose nature he was so far unaware. As from time immemorial, at the same speed at which he opened the door he raised his eyebrows. It was as though they were operated by the same mechanism.

The inspector cleared his throat and announced his sad tidings. The reaction, which his compassionate facial expression and his baritone voice were intended to allay, exceeded in dramatic intensity his worst fears. Davies emitted a long whining sound and, bending almost double, covered his face with his hands. "I knew it," he moaned. "I knew this would happen. Everything's ruined. Everything's gone."

"We are very sorry," said the inspector, looking down at the step, on which he was surprised to notice a few drops of blood. "It's a bad business."

Davies quickly pulled himself together and, reverting to his habitual air of discretion, thanked the policeman for his sympathy.

"We have the body in the van," the inspector explained, and hastily added, "wrapped up." When he had first set eyes on Mr. Davies, he had summed him up with professional alacrity as a man whose soul had been drained of all tenderness not by bitter experience but at birth. Now, for once, he was prepared to reverse his original judgment. He feared that, shown the bloodstained remains of his dumb friend, the little man might give way completely.

Davies decided that Fido's corpse should be put in the

garden shed for later burial somewhere on the grounds. At a sign from his superior, the driver of the van carried forward the dead dog wrapped in a groundsheet. Davies led the funeral cortege around the house to the back garden.

His life now seemed to him to have been a long series of undeserved misfortunes culminating in Fido's death. He felt nothing worse could happen to him. He was wrong.

The inspector's next words were, "I'm afraid there is no doubt that the dog was savage. Were you not aware of this?"

"Oh no indeed, sir. Though Fido was certainly high-spirited."

"Last night he killed someone," said the policeman. "A woman living in Leman Street."

"Not . . ." Davies managed to stop himself in time. "Not possible," he said.

"The body is in the mortuary; the marks on the neck are unmistakable."

Floundering, Davies felt for the ground beneath his feet. There was none. "I don't understand," he murmured.

"Did you ever go to Leman Street?"

"No. Well, I went there once or twice. You know." Davies would have liked to give a worldly man-to-man smile but his thin features could only manage a nervous flicker.

"Did you go there at any time yesterday evening?"

"Oh, no. At least not to the house."

All the servants at the Great House had learned never to give direct answers. They were so difficult to retract if it turned out that they had contradicted any of Lord Emms' opinions. Unfortunately the inspector found this habit not so much accommodating as shifty. Of its own accord a dog had traversed three streets to a house of ill repute and fatally mauled a woman living in a room on the second floor. To almost anybody this event would have seemed odd, but the police cannot live without crime just as surely as Raina depended on sin. To them the peculiar must be converted into the illegal. With his pallid face and evasive replies, Davies was in truth performing an action of which others are so often falsely accused by the press. He was helping the police with their inquiry. The conversation was becoming a preview for a cross-examination.

As they talked, the three men returned from the shed and came into the house through the French windows. In the drawing room the inspector paused. He did not want to tarnish his sympathetic image by appearing to be so un-English as to remain unmoved by Fido's demise, but he was determined that this slippery little man should understand that there would certainly be an inquiry into the prostitute's death and that during it, to say the very least, he would be questioned closely.

"Did the dog ever attack anyone else?" he asked.

"Oh, no. Such a thing is unthinkable." Davies had at last made a positive statement. It coincided with a glimpse, through the partially open door, of his wife creeping downstairs, one hand pressed to her bandaged eye. Chog had curled up and gone to sleep on a bed in one of the rooms upstairs. This had seemed a good moment in which to fetch the boric acid from the kitchen, where she had last bathed her wounds.

The police constable opened the door wider. "May the inspector have a word with you?" The sentence was less a question than a command.

Mrs. Davies stopped abruptly but turned slowly. By the time she faced the three men, she had passed through one hundred and eighty degrees of guilt. She looked not so much afraid as condemned.

"You've had a nasty accident," said the chief of her accusers. "I trust it is not too painful."

"Thank you, sir." She remembered not to curtsey.

"May I inquire how it happened?"

Mrs. Davies did not reply immediately. Instead she turned her gaze toward her husband. He was staring at her with almost mystical intensity. His brow was furrowed and his lips looked like the purse of a miser. There seemed to be no area of his physiognomy that was not under stress, but what she was meant to read in it she could not imagine. "I fell," she hazarded. "I fell down in the kitchen."

The policeman uttered several short clicks of sympathy and suggested that she should see a doctor. Below the bandage he noticed three scratches already becoming infected. Of these he said nothing.

Mr. Davies led the visitors to the front door as fast as his long training in decorum would permit. On the step he watched his guests until they had disappeared around the bend of the drive. Then he returned to the kitchen. "You must be mad," he hissed. "Take all that stuff and go upstairs where you can look after . . ." Unable to bring himself to mention Chog, he jerked his cobra head toward the ceiling. To his amazement his wife answered him back.

"Yes. I am mad," she said. "And so would you be if you had this." In spite of the pain the action caused her, she ripped the bandage from her head and pointed to her eyelid. It was scarlet.

To her surprise and relief she was not put to the effort of defying her husband and going in search of medical aid. Within an hour a doctor she had never seen before came to the house. As she asked him no questions, he saw no reason to mention that he had been sent by the police. Unlike her, he removed the bandage with the greatest care. When the worst was revealed, he surveyed the damage through narrowed eyes and drew in a long breath through clenched teeth. He made no comment on the nature of the injury, nor did he inquire about its cause. "You should have had this seen to at once," he scolded gently. The patient was beginning to realize the wisdom of this statement. The entire side of her face had started to feel hot and painful. Nevertheless, when it was suggested that there was now no other course but for her to go to the hospital, she became agitated. She had never been in a public building in her life. To calm her, the physician explained that he would give her a letter which she could hand to whomever spoke to her. She herself need say nothing.

Mrs. Davies was touched by the doctor's quiet solicitude, but her husband, who regarded him as a spy, was frightened and angry. Until recently his abiding contempt for his wife had always been expressed by a weary condescension, but lately he had become openly hostile. This had not caused her to retreat from him still further. On the contrary, provoked by pain and fear, she had begun to abandon her customary stoical silence and to answer back. It could not be said that she had decided to engage him in battle; she spoke in a tone of supplicatory self-defense. "I only said he was nice," she pleaded.

"He is not 'nice,' as you put it," Davies explained laboriously. "That man sent him here not to cure you but to find out what was really wrong with you. And you let him in," he added in a louder tone.

"All the same, I'm glad he came. I feel a lot better," Mrs. Davies mumbled, gently patting the clean bandage. "Doesn't that count for anything?"

"They will prosecute us," her accuser croaked. "Don't you understand that?"

"What for? What have we done?" Mrs. Davies looked at her husband and then revised her question. "What have I done?"

Mr. Davies saw that she was going to cry again. This was something else that in the past she had seldom done. "On account of the dog," he said more quietly. "He says it was savage."

"That's not my fault."

"I know it isn't, but *they* don't. What's worse, they don't care. They'll have us both in jail, if you're not careful."

"Prison!"

"You know what the police are like."

She didn't. Until she entered the service of Lord Emms, she had lived in the country. The local bobby had been a joke.

"There will be an inquest," Davies prophesied. He was making a great effort not to hit his wife.

"What's that?"

"The same as when his lordship died." Davies had forgotten that on that occasion she had been ill or had feigned illness. "An inquiry into everything."

"About Fido's death?"

"About hers."

"Oh, no." The very idea of being questioned by anyone in authority made Mrs. Davies feel defeated. Whenever Lord Emms or even her ladyship had demanded an explanation for something she had done wrong, she had only been able to say that she couldn't think how the accident had happened. Objects of value fell to the floor or even ran away and hid themselves; brightly burning fires went out the moment her back was turned; and on the newly swept carpet crumbs appeared like mushrooms. Now someone she had never seen had died in a street along which she had never walked and people were going to ask her to account for it. Would the cost of this tragedy also be deducted from her wages?

While husband and wife wrangled, they heard above their

heads the patter of tiny feet. Automatically Mrs. Davies rose and went to the bottom of the stairs.

"The first thing we've got to do now," her husband called after her, "is to get rid of you-know-who."

Mrs. Davies turned toward him. She was too frightened to speak and only stood staring at his eyes. Immediately he realized that he should not have mentioned this particular chore. The woman was now too hysterical to be of any help. He had spoken only from a lifelong habit of involving her in anything that was at all unpleasant.

The day after this conversation Mrs. Davies woke early and, in spite of feeling unwell, went downstairs immediately. Her husband stayed in bed pretending to be asleep until she was out of the room. Their relationship was now so bad that they spent as little time together as possible. In the kitchen she lit the fire and prepared a meal for Chog. On this occasion she indulged him limitlessly, placing before him porridge, two boiled eggs, several slices of bread and butter cut into narrow strips, and two mugs of milk. While he gulped down everything she offered, she sat opposite him smiling but the tears ran down her face unheeded.

After breakfast she took the daily paper up to her husband so as to keep him in bed as long as possible and, from a drawer in their room, fetched a thick woolen cardigan. Downstairs again, she put this on the child, rolled up the sleeves, and tied a piece of thick string around his waist. On such a small body the garment looked like a monk's habit.

There was a row of hooks sticking out of the mantelshelf above the kitchen range. On several of them hung keys of different sizes and shapes. One of these she put in her pocket. All her movements had suddenly taken on unusual precision. She crouched down in front of the child, took his hands and, turning, placed them around her neck from behind. Chog enjoyed this maneuver and at once began to lick her ears. Lifting the child, Mrs. Davies struggled to her feet and left the house quietly by the side door.

Trying to carry her burden as though they were playing a game, she crossed the cold lawn and, stooping low under the unpruned fruit trees, passed through the small wilderness that lay beyond. The child stopped nuzzling her neck to pluck at the branches above his head. Presently they came to the gate with the wire netting that the contractor had affixed above the fence even though Davies had considered it unnecessary. Here she succeeded in detaching herself from the child's embrace so that she might use both hands to turn the key in the rusty lock. The ditch that ran along the other side of the fence was at this time of year a small stream. Mrs. Davies led the child across the flat, turf-covered bridge. He was delighted with these new, rural surroundings and longed to explore them. When, fearing that he would fall into the water, Mrs. Davies refused to let go of his hand, he bit her wrist. The gesture was intended playfully, but the pain was sharp enough to make her relinquish her grasp. She decided to entice him away from the danger by moving slowly up the rising ground of the field. The child ran to her and away again several times until, on the skyline, he noticed a sheep. He stood stock-still for a moment, shuddering from head to foot. Then very cautiously, he walked toward it. Mrs. Davies moved with equal stealth back to the stream. Without ever taking her eyes from the odd little figure in the tall grass, she reentered the garden and locked the gate.

There, as though she were a prisoner, she stood with her hands on the wire netting until Chog had disappeared from view.

Exeunt

When she returned to the house, she found her husband sitting in the kitchen. Hunger had overcome his reluctance to confront his wife. She made breakfast for him and, without looking at him, announced that she was going to Ravenage Hospital. He made no attempt to dissuade her. At that moment he felt that all the harm she could do was done.

In fact she went to the bishop's palace. A new member of his grace's staff opened the back door, went to look for the housekeeper, and returned to say that she was out, shopping. Mrs. Davies believed this. She left a message and set off to face her ordeal. She had not presumed to ask Mrs. Adie to visit her in the hospital. She only hoped that the information that she had gone there would prompt her friend to come.

Presumably patients are always made to wait for hours in the hospital because it is hoped that, after a while, their fatigue will become harder to bear than the pains of their illness and they will go away again. This ruse could never work on Mrs. Davies. It would fail not because she held strong views about her rights to medical attention or because she thought that, without help, she might die. A social superior had given her a letter to deliver. This was a mission that only death could prevent her from carrying out.

Contrary to what she had imagined on her way to the hospital, she had nothing to fear from the cruelty of the nurses. They did not bully her; they ignored her. It was the other people sitting in the corridor who were so hostile . . . albeit indirectly. Among these was the young lady from the newspaper shop. As soon as Mrs. Davies sat down, the girl, leaning forward so as to be able to fire across the chests of four strangers, shouted, "We all heard about your dog. Such a shame. But with a woman like that, what can you expect. They've got no feelings—can't have."

Sensing an opportunity to moralize, the three women and one man that sat between Mrs. Davies and her inquisitor moved their heads from side to side like spectators at a tennis match. The rally was short-lived. Mrs. Davies managed a flicker of a gracious smile and then returned to looking at the floor in front of her. She did not explain that it was not the woman that had killed the dog but the reverse.

When at last a girl smelling strongly of formaldehyde called her name, she was relieved to be able to escape the stares of those about her.

She was examined by a surgeon and told that a small operation would be necessary. She was warned that the treatment would take a little longer than usual as efforts must be made to reduce the inflammation. Mrs. Davies accepted the news meekly.

She was passing from the habitual timidity with which she addressed strangers into an unnatural acquiescence. When she was admitted to the hospital, the nurses who attended to her had the impression that the patient was altogether unaware of her surroundings for minutes at a time. The usual efforts made to frighten her by withholding information about her progress were in vain. When her husband visited her, Mrs. Davies roused herself sufficiently to ask for a few personal belongings that she had forgotten to bring with her. Davies agreed to perform the requested errand but with bad grace; he had only visited the damned hospital because, once she was out of sight, he felt that he had no control over his wife's indiscretion. He had wanted to warn her to say nothing either to the staff or to other patients. He also wished to disconcert her by telling her that the inquest he had dreaded was now a certainty. He implied that whatever happened during it would be her fault. By the time he had overcome his reluctance sufficiently to bring her the objects for which she had asked, it was time for her to leave.

A letter had been brought to the Great House while she was away. It was lying on the kitchen mantelshelf when she returned home. If Davies had known what grief it would cause his wife, he would not have omitted to take it to her in the hospital.

Mrs. Adie did not think it sufficient that her moral standards should be implied by her general behavior; she wished them to be stated. In prose of astonishing formality, she wrote that she hoped she was still Mrs. Davies' friend. She was sincerely sorry about all the misfortunes that had recently befallen her but felt that her own position in his grace's household required her to set an example to the younger members of his staff. Therefore, at any rate for the time being, she much regretted that it would be more circumspect if Mrs. Davies discontinued the visits that in the past had been so enjoyable.

The note contained so many long and unfamiliar words that Mrs. Davies could not understand it. She was compelled to hand it to her husband. He read the contents aloud in imitation of Mrs. Adie's voice, which, though it lacked the rasping irritability, was so like his own—the same passionless melody sung a fifth higher.

As he laid the azure, deckle-edged page on the table, he said, "You had to do it, didn't you? You had to confide in that woman and tell her all our business."

Mrs. Davies had told her friend nothing. Mrs. Adie knew more about the scandal and had known it sooner than she, but Mrs. Davies made no logical attempt to defend herself from her husband's accusations. "I just wanted to have a friend," she said. "That's all."

Davies genuinely could not understand this. For once the divergence of opinion was not on principle. He cleaned the brass and the silver exactly as he had done when Lord Emms was alive and he now also pretended to tend the garden. These domestic rituals adequately filled his days. He had no hobbies; he took no holidays; he needed no cronies. He really believed that he could form an unbiased and detailed opinion of the outer world by reading a daily paper from cover to cover.

"I haven't anyone," his wife went on. Then, in a quieter but more desperate voice, she added, "No one."

When, as now, things were at their worst, she thought of Chog, but she never went to the wire gate. She did not dare. If he were waiting for her on the other side of the fence, she would be unable to refrain from allowing him back into the garden, even though she sincerely believed that her husband would murder him.

From this prospect she revolted with her entire soul.

The extermination of Lord Emms' pets had been an expedient in which she had felt compelled to take part for the sake of her livelihood and the preservation of things as they had always been. Now she was less sure that this state of affairs was worth maintaining. Looking back, which she hated to do, she realized that Davies had not shared her repugnance. She remembered that he had kept up a whispered banter with his victims, giving them poison as though it were a treat, killing them as if it were a game. To him, doing away with Chog might merely be a bigger test of his ingenuity.

Except for Mrs. Davies, no one in Ravenage thought much about the child. Mr. Davies thought that he had escaped and was slightly relieved. Those neighbors of the Sylvesters who had been carefully told that Chog had gone to stay with his grandparents told those who knew nothing. At present what occupied the gossips most was the bizarre nature of Raina's death.

Even the police believed—or seemed to believe—the popular explanation of Chog's absence. The disappearance that angered the inspector was that of Mr. Sylvester. His escape

had been made possible by the amount of blood on his clothes.

When the constable, whom Davies had seen sauntering to the scene of the crime, had investigated the situation, he asked the husband of the deceased to accompany him to the police station. Mr. Sylvester had spread out his pale hands and looked down at his suit. To the inexperienced policeman there seemed no reason not to allow him to change his clothes. "I'll be quite a while," Mr. Sylvester explained. "I'll have to take off every stitch I've got on." He wiggled his toes in his blood-filled suede shoes and made a grimace of disgust. "Will it be all right if I come down in half an hour?"

The policeman agreed to this arrangement. He had been surprised at the calmness with which the widower had surveyed the corpse of his wife but, as the marks on her throat were so obviously the work of the dog, he could not at the moment think of any pretext for an arrest.

After entering the back room to change his clothes, Raina's husband was never for certain seen again. He couldn't afford to be. He had been in trouble with the law before, and more than once. The dead woman was not the first prostitute on whose earnings he had lived; she was only the most dedicated, the funniest, and the least greedy for money. On the occasion of his most recent arrest, he had given his occupation as gambling. "There was no gamble here," the magistrate's clerk had observed. "This women was a dead cert."

At the inquest on Raina's death, the coroner explained more than once that the proceedings were not a trial. Whatever distinction he was trying to make was no comfort to Mrs. Davies. She was afraid. The only circumstance that was any solace to her was that her husband would be asked to give evidence before she did. She hoped his example would show her how to conduct herself.

It did no such thing. Mr. Davies' neat appearance and respectful manner made a good first impression but, when he spoke, the only thing that was clear about his testimony was that he was hiding something. To the coroner, as to the police, it was a matter of indifference whether Davies had visited the dead woman's flat on one occasion or every night of his life. The savage nature of the dog was the only thing that concerned them, and in this connection its keeper had nothing to fear. The attacks on Mrs. Davies and on Raina had occurred within half an hour of one another. It would have been quite easy to say that a previously docile animal had gone suddenly and unaccountably mad. It was because no such words were uttered that a statement from Mrs. Davies was sought.

With the help of an official, Mrs. Davies managed to reach the stand without stumbling, but from the moment she was asked to turn and face the room she heard almost nothing more that was said to her. Lifting her gaze momentarily from the floor, she had caught sight of Mr. Minguillan. At once her thoughts, on which she had been trying to impose some order, were thrown into confusion. She had known that as soon as the news of Fido's death reached him, he would appear, but she had tried to put the thought from her. The sight of this baleful man struck her like a physical blow. She drew in her breath so sharply that she choked and had to be given a glass of water. To her the lawyer personified desolation. Though she had come to hate every aspect of her present way of life, she needed its protection against the outer world which had changed so much while she had remained unaltered and unalterable. She was told that she might sit but made no move until a chair was pushed toward her from behind. Then she sat down heavily, clasping her hands tightly in her lap. Her head fell forward until nothing was visible beneath the crown of her black straw hat. The coroner asked if she felt all right. She made no reply. When her position remained unchanged for half a minute, it was thought that she might be concentrating on her replies, even praying. Finally the court realized that she was crying. She was led back to her seat. She had given no evidence; she had said not a word.

Outside the coroner's office, the Davieses found Mr. Minguillan waiting for them. Though they protested out of fear of him rather than politeness, he escorted them back to the Great House. As on previous occasions, he made a painstaking tour of inspection of all the rooms; he uttered the usual muted praise for the way the place had been kept up. All that differentiated this visit from others before it was that throughout the proceedings the Davieses stood side by side in the hall and that, though they went into the dining room to receive their wages, Mr. Minguillan was offered no coffee. He did not remark on this omission.

They were given a month's notice and for the first time they were told on what day of the following month the next visit would occur. On that occasion they would be given free railway tickets to whatever part of the British Isles they wished to go. This kindness was bestowed upon them to ensure that they did not leave before the lawyer checked the inventory for the last time.

When their visitor had departed, the Davieses returned to the kitchen in silence. Ever since the reading of Lord Emms' will, Mrs. Davies had wondered from time to time what would have happened to her if Fido had died of that first dose of arsenic that her husband had administered. She had mentioned her fears to Mr. Davies, but he had altogether refused to indulge in such morbid fancies. Now it made no difference; both were equally crushed.

While she prepared their midday meal, Mrs. Davies spoke occasionally, but in a toneless voice and only of trivial things. Seated at the table, she ate nothing, even of the tiny portion she had allotted to herself. It was not until her husband had finished eating that she turned her face toward him and with great deliberation asked, "How much money have we got altogether?"

From the laborious way in which he drew in his breath before speaking, she knew that her savings were gone, but she waited. "Well, you know," Davies began, picking some crumbs from the tablecloth and placing them on his plate, "things have been difficult lately. Everything has gone up in price."

"But I've always done the shopping," his wife pointed out. "Except for the few days I was in hospital."

Altering his course, Davies tried blaming Mr. Minguillan. He accused him of being mean in spite of the fact that he obviously had everything anyone could wish for. "He's probably spending on himself what is rightfully hours."

"Fido's," said Mrs. Davies quietly. The word silenced her husband for a moment, so she went on. "What about the money we'd saved before we'd ever heard of Mr. Minguillan?"

"Well, it's like this."

"Even before the master died, we had something."

"It's hard to explain finances to a woman."

Mrs. Davies rose to her feet, abruptly pushing her chair back across the uneven stone floor. Its rasping sound expressed a little of her contempt. She knew the money had been spent on "that woman," but where it had gone had now ceased to matter. For a long moment she stood looking down at her husband. "Twenty-five years," she said. "Wasted."

These were the last words she ever uttered.

She took the plates, the cutlery, the saucepans into the scullery and washed everything up. Then she washed the tea towel as well and hung it out to dry. When she returned to the kitchen, her husband avoided looking at her. This made it easy for her to take the key to the wire gate from its hook without being noticed. Not knowing why, she walked through the entire house making sure that everything was tidy. Then she left by the side door and crossed the garden to the back fence.

She could not help thinking of Chog. In spite of all that had happened, she longed to find him waiting for her and to hug him, but she knew that this was an idle daydream. It was weeks since she had watched him disappear over the brow of the hill.

Leaving the gate open, she passed into the field and stood for a long time staring at the stream. It was fast sinking into the ditch as it did every summer. She walked beside it searching for a place where the water was deep enough for her purpose. Several hundred yards downstream was a second bridge as low as the one she had just crossed but so choked with weeds that the rivulet, unable to pass easily underneath it, had widened into a tiny lake. On the bank, Mrs. Davies sat down and slowly drew off her boots and stockings. As she surveyed the sluggish brown water a thought drifted unbidden into her mind: the tortoise would have lived forever.

When she stepped into the stream, it felt surprisingly cold to her warm flesh but she forced herself to lie face downward in it and to take a deep breath of this fierce element. With all her soul she longed to die but, in spite of everything it had suffered, her body wanted to live. After only a few seconds her instinct compelled her to lift her head. To her bewilderment she found that she was unable to do this. The current had carried her in among the reeds under the bridge. At last the ineptitude that, all her life, had caused her so much humiliation came to her aid. She drowned.

Raina's body, which in life had been the object of such monstrous desires, such hissing contempt, so many bizarre

conjectures, in death was hardly more than a nuisance. She was buried with a minimum of ceremony. The gossips of Ravenage turned their attention to a different series of rumors.

When Chog, abandoned by Mrs. Davies, had proceeded up the field behind Lord Emms' house, he had at first been unaware that he was now alone. He walked slowly through the grass that was nearly as tall as he, then broke into a run with a curious gait—leaning forward, his neck outstretched, his fingertips just touching the ground. At the top of the hill he found that the animal he had seen from below was one of a flock. At first he was delighted with their companionship and darted to and fro among the sheep uttering hoarse cries of laughter. When they would not play and showed that they were afraid of him, some of the old feelings of contempt that he had felt for the landlord's cat came over him. He was trying to climb onto the back of one of them when a farmer's boy appeared, waving his arms and shouting. Chog ran away and hid. As yet he was only dimly aware of the danger he was in, but his life as an outlaw had begun.

Being the child of a mixed marriage or, rather, the bastard of mixed parentage, he was in a state of perpetual confusion. At night he slept fitfully in barns and granaries, frightened and alone. At such times he cried out for his mother, though she had shown him no affection and very little attention. By day his mood changed rapidly. He was overjoyed with the sunshine, the wind in the hills, and all the multifarious smells of summer.

In an ecstasy of oneness with the earth, he would fling himself on the ground and roll about with his legs in the air.

Inevitably, this totally free existence could not last forever. Rumors spread; thefts were reported; the bones of chickens were found strewn about farmyards; dustbins were overturned. Because his presence was known rather than seen, he became an object of superstitious fear. The greatest mystery was that when farmers tried to track down this enigmatic quarry with the aid of dogs, as often as not the dogs disappeared. Some never returned at all; others slunk home several days later having suffered an unaccountable personality change. They were no longer obedient or even friendly.

Part of the difficulty of catching Chog arose from the fact that descriptions of him varied widely. The farmer's boy who had glimpsed him in the distance among the sheep said that it was some kind of brown woolly animal that had been attempting to mount a ewe. Some children whom Chog had approached at a picnic agreed that he was older than themselves but said that he was smaller. When pressed for more details about his appearance, they began to cry and could not be questioned further. A woman who found him foraging in her pigbin described him as an unkempt youth.

As the myth increased in improbability, its subject moved farther out onto the moors. For a few days it seemed that the threat of his presence had evaporated altogether. The townsfolk began to talk of other things.

Then, quite suddenly, on a day so fair that even the countryside around Ravenage looked beautiful, Lady Emms' nephew saw Chog crouching in a mustard field near where the body of Mrs. Davies still lay hidden. Immediately the farmer put his collie to the chase. Though this animal had recently been most recalcitrant, it set off at once. To his owner's amazement, as the dog drew near, Chog stood up and beckoned. For a moment the collie paused, absolutely still; then it approached its new master and together they disappeared over the hill. As he watched this curious incident, the farmer became aware that the entire district was full of dogs. From distant towns, neighboring hamlets, and isolated barns, a four-footed army was converging on Ravenage. Within an hour the whole town was beset by the sound of hysterical barking. Even Davies heard it as he stood alone watching from the bolted windows of his dead master's house.

If the dogs had been without a leader, Davies might have survived their attack. They would simply have stormed the Great House; he would have locked himself in an upper room until help arrived. This was not to be.

The invaders were under the command of a mind more human, therefore both more devious and more daring, than theirs. The entire army passed, as silent as Assyrians, through the gate that Mrs. Davies had left open, and in short, sharp dashes from one bush to another, reached the very walls of the house. When their silence had lasted almost half an hour, Davies' curiosity overcame his caution. He crept downstairs, went into the living room, and looked through those French windows which gave him the widest view of the garden. As soon as his parchment face approached the light, as if out of nowhere, Chog sprang at him. Trying to shield himself from a rain of broken glass, Davies tottered back, all the while striking savagely at his assailant with Lord Emms' walking stick. He managed to reach the hall, but it proved impossible to shut the door. A huge mongrel sheepdog had jumped almost un-scathed through the opening in the window made by his leader and now he wedged himself in the doorway. At each violent effort of Davies to shut the door, this animal's ribs cracked. It yelped but it did not budge. After a few seconds, the man retreated and a torrent of dogs poured into the hall. They caught up with their enemy just as he began to climb the stairs.

When the police finally arrived, they found almost every-thing in the hall broken. The floor was slimy with blood and the excrement of dogs, who had now begun to fight among them-selves as, growling continuously, they shredded the flesh of their victim.

Davies lay on the lowest step, his suit torn from his body, his face ripped from his skull.

Chog had got no farther than the living-room doorway. No decision whether to shoot him or take him to the hospital had to be made. While this point was being argued by the farmers and policemen, he died of his wounds.

· CHOG ·

The End